THE WORD OF THE WIVES

THE WORD OF THE WIVES

Monologues from the unheard women of the Bible

Abby Guinness
and Michele Guinness

Authentic

Copyright © 2010 Abby Guinness and Michele Guinness

16 15 14 13 12 11 10   7 6 5 4 3 2 1

First published 2010 by Authentic Media Limited
Milton Keynes
www.authenticmedia.co.uk
Company Registration No: 7101487

The right of Abby Guinness and Michele Guinness to be identified as
the Authors of this Work has been asserted by them in accordance
with the Copyright, Designs and Patents Act 1988

The material in this book is free to photocopy

British Library Cataloguing in Publication Data

A catalogue record for this book is available from the British Library

978-1-85078-872-0

Cover Design by Philip Miles
Printed in Great Britain by Cox and Wyman, Reading

Contents

Introduction

Extracts from selected e-mails, 2002–2009

Hi Mum
Attached a piece I've just written. Not sure if I'll ever perform it, but when the muse descends . . . Let me know what you think.

Hi Abby
I love Mrs Noah. I laughed out loud. What gave you the idea?

Actually, I got it from you (along with the recent torrential rain). A couple of years ago, I saw you flouncing across the church stage on Easter Day in a hideous nylon negligee from Marks and Spencer. You were playing Mrs Caiaphas, I believe.

Fancy you remembering that. I hoped no one would! It was the plight of the poor minister that drove me to it. The despair on your dad's face on Good Friday that said,

'I've been so busy with Holy Week I haven't thought about Sunday yet. How are we going to approach the story in a new and engaging way for all-comers?' We'd not long since been on a trip to Israel and visited the House of the Sadducees in Jerusalem. I couldn't believe my eyes when there in a glass cabinet was the make-up of the High Priest's wife. I thought, 'Well, what do you know, Mrs Caiaphas was as vain as I am.' And of course, being married to the minister, I could really play on being Mrs High Priest!

I liked hearing it from her point of view. And I was drawn to the ease of it – the simplicity of a complete story without a cast of thousands in elaborate costumes, who'd never turned up for rehearsals and then forgot their lines. And of course, it was a novel take on the resurrection. Everyone was mesmerized. But that might have been the negligee.

Two years on . . .

Hi Mum
Mrs Noah finally got an outing! I performed it for Rob (Lacey) after a couple of *street bible* extracts. When he asked me who wrote it, and I told him I had, he said, 'It must be nice to work with good writing for a change!' Made me smile.

Great to hear Mrs Noah went down well. I've attached one for you. This last Easter, I metamorphosed into Mrs

Zebedee, the mother of James and John. No negligee this time. The roles I'm comfortable in are getting older – but hey ho, that's inevitable. What is it they say about there being no good parts for women past a certain age?

The parts for women of *any* age are not that juicy or plentiful. Most of the actresses I know would understand why the early Pharisees felt the need for that daily prayer you told me about: 'I thank you God that I was not born a Gentile, a slave, a leper or a woman.' Although I've always thought it was a bit on the harsh side.

I think it was pure relief that they didn't have to face the trials and heartache that came with being a woman. I can think of a contemporary alternative: 'I thank you, God, that my daughter has not become a prostitute, beggar, writer or actress.'

Touché! I can't say there aren't times I would rather have ended up earning a comfortable living whilst saving the world, but this seems to be where my skills and passions have led me . . . and anyway, you started it!

Four years on . . .

Hey Mum

How was Easter? The creative and all-age events here went well. I could probably now add herding cattle to my CV. The big productions are fun, but monologues are getting more appealing by the minute. I've done a few more and been testing them out on friends in the biz. Steve Stickley (at Footprints) particularly warmed to the women. He wants to see more of them (as it were!). I think he's right, there's something in it. Perhaps there's a whole collection . . .

The idea of a whole collection of women is exciting, but will it look like some kind of feminist drive?

I know what you mean, but I don't think gender should be an issue. These women open windows on the Bible that are just as intriguing for men as for women. We're telling the same stories, but from a different point of view. It's the men who tend to get the headlines, but if husbands and wives are 'one flesh' (Gen. 2:24), then the women must've felt every joy and pain along the journey. The better-known women have already had their stories told; I'd quite like to find the unheard ones.
I love finding a new way into a familiar story, one that can aid our engagement with it. I'll do a few more and see where we get to.

One year on . . .

Hi Abby
Thanks so much for doing Mrs Zacchaeus at the conference yesterday. It makes such a difference when an audience can see and experience the theme, not just hear about it.

It's funny that I didn't see it before; it was only when you were in the middle that I realized how contemporary these women are. I was watching the audience and I could see that Mrs Zac's story was having an impact on a few of the women that I had never anticipated – women who must have been longing for years for their husbands to change. But being told we shouldn't try to change our men, they had resigned themselves to living with someone who was far from what they hoped he would be when they married him.

It started me thinking about all kinds of situations that confront women today – loneliness, abuse, neglect, fear, compromise, and just plain being taken for granted. And there's just as much of it in the Bible as in the world today.

It's pretty astounding, isn't it? For thousands of years the Bible has been read by those of some religion or none, scholars and peasants alike, and because it's concerned with what it means to be human, it's still entirely contemporary and relevant to people of all descriptions.

I'm glad Mrs Zac struck a chord. I hope she's not the only one who does. I love the freedom of stewing biblical history and fiction and exploring what it could mean to us now. I don't need or want to 'contribute' to Scripture in any way, but I enjoy finding new ways of recounting it. And these characters are allowing us to do that. With nothing but a bit of background reading and the creator's favourite question, 'What if?' I'm sure people will notice that I'm not a biblical expert, just an enthusiast with a (hefty) dollop of artistic licence.

Can you send me Mrs Caiaphas? And throw me in any extras if you get time. I'll get onto the rest. I've attached Mrs Jonah for you to look at.

I feel like I've met Mrs Jonah before! What I like is that by letting your imagination roam, you end up wrestling and engaging with the Bible differently and, dare I say it, a bit more deeply. And it sure beats – I mean, complements – a talk!

How would you encourage people to use them?

People can use them however they want to . . . read and ponder them, buy them as a gift, leave them on the coffee table as a conversation starter, read them aloud to others or, even better, learn and perform them wherever they can. I think they work in place of the reading in church, or alongside the reading or sermon, in schools, or anywhere people are looking at a Bible story. (We'll have to negotiate the legalities for professional performers, but if the audience is not paying, and it's not being recorded or sold, then people should feel free to use the material if they credit the authors.)

Or, those shy of performing could book me (or both of us) to perform individual pieces or a whole show, live at their event or venue. If we put them on a DVD and CD as well, it will help people get an idea of how they are in performance. I must get on to that. I can post the details on my website once they're available. It's up and running now, have I told you?

Check out www.livingandactive.co.uk

We're gathering steam . . .

I challenge you to get it done by the end of the year. (Seeing as you started seven years ago!) Do you mind me sticking my oar in?

So long as I can stick mine in your pieces too. I know I'm the drama writer, but I'm grateful for the extra material. And I value your input.

Here are the few I've done. Send me the edited versions of these and the other pieces when they're ready and I'll cast my beady eye over them. Thank goodness for email.

I reckon the Bible would be a different kettle of fish if email had been around sooner. Look forward to seeing you at Christmas when we can try out a few more. I'm Miss Shepherd, you're Mrs Balthasar. All we need now is to get them written . . .

How to Read These Monologues

Reading a script is different from reading a narrative. You will have to do a little work to get the most out of it.

People don't explain or say things aloud in the same way as they write them down (unless they are lecturing.) Conversation is less descriptive and less obvious. We instinctively dig around the words for meaning, using tone of voice, body language and personality. You will enjoy, appreciate and understand these pieces more easily if you remember they are direct speech. Every line is birthed in a character's head and spoken through their experience and emotions. It creates layers of meaning. They take on life in performance.

That's not to say you can't enjoy reading them as much as seeing them acted. As you read, give the character a personality and a voice, even in your head. Imagine them speaking aloud. What do they look like? How do they sound? What are they thinking?

In some of the pieces, the character is talking directly to someone else who may or may not be responding. Even though we only hear one side of the conversation, you can freely imagine what the other person is saying and mentally 'fill in the gaps'.

It might also be that some of these pieces are easier to grasp when read alongside the Bible passage they are based on.

I hope you will find the extra effort of engaging your imagination worth it, as it will unlock more than you see on the page.

Abby Guinness
April 2010

Notes for Performers

These monologues are meant not only to be read, but to be performed. There are all sorts of occasions you might find to do so. If you're raring to go and know all about performing, great, you can skip this chapter. If, after reading thi, you're still nervous or have queries, you could drop me a line via my website, www.livingand-active.co.uk. I'm happy to advise or come and do a workshop to get you started. But the first port of call is: be brave. You learn what works by doing it. So give it a try!

Approaching the text

There are some ideas about character and delivery in the introduction to each piece. There are also a few stage directions within the scripts. I have, however, kept both of these to a minimum. They can be distracting and spoil the flow of the story, but more than that, I think it's important for each performer to bring the monologue to life in their own way. If I were to be overly specific, it might limit what you felt you could do. Ultimately, your interpretation of the monologue is as valid as the writer's own. Any script can be adapted to fit your purpose and your resources. What you bring to it enhances the piece and becomes part of the finished product.

All you need to create theatre is people, in a space, with a story. Simplicity and minimalism work well with these monologues. The words and your delivery of them should be the main focus. Good delivery comes from knowing and communicating the character and their story clearly. To do that, preparation is vital. You may find it useful to read the Bible passage the piece is based on. It could give you extra clues. Then, as you spend time with the script, you should spend some time answering important questions relating to the story, the character and the listener. What happens in the piece? What happens before and after it? Is there a turning point or epiphany? Where is the climax? What is being said in the words and in the intention behind them? What is the character's attitude? Does she mean what she is saying? What is she thinking and feeling? Who is she speaking to? Why them? Why now? Once discovered, how are you going to communicate these things clearly? The text itself and the introduction will give you clues, but you have to make decisions of your own.

Think, too, about your audience. The pieces will appeal to different people. Consider who is watching, and how your performance fits in with what else is going on. Those with little or no Bible knowledge will find it easier to connect with someone like Mrs Noah than one of the less familiar characters.

Casting and character

If I were to say that Mrs Noah is a 57-year-old woman with wild, greying hair and a Bristolian accent, it might make someone who doesn't fit that bill reluctant to play her. I believe anyone can play any of these roles regardless of age, accent, appearance or even gender. Having said that, deciding on a description of them for yourself will help you play them. In some cases, I have suggested age and accent, but purely as an insight into what I was imagining as I wrote. In reality, the character looks and sounds however you imagine them when you read their words.

Physicality is a great way to expand and deepen a character. As you watch people, you'll notice that we all walk and move differently. Think about the posture of your character; is she proud and straight-backed? Is she an impatient fidget? Is she self-conscious and slouching?

Making decisions about the character will enrich your performance, but don't fall into the trap of creating a caricature. It is much better to be a real person, even if that means performing the character as a version of yourself. We all have character and depth, but none of us are stereotypes. The best actors make great use of subtlety.

In a monologue, it is particularly important to decide who you are addressing. Your relationship with them is hugely important. Many of these monologues have a specified listener – someone to whom the character is speaking. That person is not physically present, but the audience must believe they are. Leave spaces for the lines they would speak, and 'listen' to them. You should know exactly what they are saying because it affects your response (although you need not always make the pause one of realistic length, as that would slow the action too much). If you are clear where that person is standing or sitting, and how they are responding to you, the audience will find it easy to imagine them.

The pieces that don't have a particular listener give you some freedom. You could choose to invent one, or to speak directly to the audience. (Mrs Ten allows you to speak freely to whatever crowd is actually gathered.) Remember only to address the audience directly if that is your plan; it will confuse them if you're meant to be speaking to a particular individual, yet talk to them. If you have a willing second actor, it would be very easy in some of these pieces to write in the missing lines and create a duologue.

Props, costume and staging

You might find one or two props are essential. Mrs John has a letter (or manuscript) in her hand; Mrs Hosea pulls a note out of her pocket or bag. Things like that are easy to find or make. Remember too that theatre can communicate without needing realism. For Mrs Adam and Mrs John, you can use a bundle of blankets to represent a baby. However, beware of miming props – it is very difficult to be clearly understood. It's usually better to use something real, representative, or not at all.

Some props will give you something to do if you're feeling at a loss for movements. It's perfectly acceptable to decide that Mrs Potiphar is eating grapes, or Mrs Solomon is sewing. There are no rules!

These pieces certainly don't need the support of a full wardrobe. You could perform them in your own clothes very successfully. It probably helps to wear something comfortable that won't distract you or the audience from what you're saying. Or you can try and dress faithfully to the character, if you wish.

I'm a fan of using one or two small items to suggest a costume. These need not be complex or time-specific. They simply help to suggest what type of person this is, or what she has been doing. Actually, this serves the performer as much as the audience, because it helps you to feel the part. For example, Miss Shepherd may wear a big coat, because she spends most of her time outside in the cold night. Putting on some fashionable high heels might help you to feel like Mrs Caiaphas, who is constantly aware of her image.

Similarly, staging can be easily suggested rather than fully realized. Mrs Abraham is coming to a parents' evening; a wooden or plastic school chair would be enough to make that environment familiar. Ms X is in a police cell; putting her at a table could help to represent that scene.

Be aware that if you choose to sit down for your performance, it will make it harder for people to see you, unless your stage is substantially raised above the audience. Standing works best if sight lines are difficult. Try to perform somewhere that is visible to as many people in the room as possible.

Microphones are not essential. The voice is more powerful than you might think; you won't need to shout to be heard. Have a practice beforehand to test the right volume for your venue. If there's an echo, you will have to slow down and annunciate even more clearly. If you do have a microphone, remember it will not do all the work for you. The best sound quality comes when you use the strength of your voice and let the microphone boost it, rather than relying on it completely.

Rehearsal and delivery

However experienced you are, it is important to rehearse. As you practise, you can use verbs to explore how delivery affects the piece. In each moment, what is the character doing? Is she wondering? Is she deciding, realizing, or questioning? Is she belittling, encouraging, or nagging? Trying different ways of delivering the lines aloud will help you find what works.

Make sure you've delivered the piece fluidly many times before you attempt a public performance. Using a test audience of one or two friends will help to reduce your nerves before a bigger crowd, and will give you some indication of where people might laugh, and how they might respond.

I'm often asked, 'How do you remember all those lines?' The fact is, I do because I have to! You just have to knuckle down and do it. The encouragement is that everyone is capable of learning lines if they put aside the time. And the more often you do it, the easier you'll find it. If you understand the lines and know the story they tell, you will find it easier to remember them. Knowing what happens in the story will also equip you to approximate the lines until you're back on track in case of a blank. I think it is worth making the effort. It takes time, but there is something magical for the audience when the performer is fully immersed in the piece. It takes on a life of its own in that moment, and can live in the memory for a long time.

However, I also think these pieces work well read aloud. If you don't have the time to learn lines, reading is certainly a strong second best. When reading to an audience, you should prepare in the same way, and perform as much as you would without the script in front of you. Make sure you have practised aloud in the way you will be performing, because the amount of breath you use changes with your volume and intonation. You might like to mark on the script any pauses you want to leave, or good places to take a breath. Practise the bits that make you stumble – you will eventually get your mouth around them! Try a few different ways of delivering it to find the best one.

Some people like to read with the script in their hand, others prefer a lectern or podium to rest on. Find a way you will be comfortable. It's good to look up as much as possible when reading, to connect with your listeners. I find it really helpful to photocopy or retype the piece into larger print, and use double spacing, which makes it easier to find your place when you glance down.

Finally, and most importantly, enjoy yourself. If you appear unprepared or tentative, the audience will worry on your behalf. If you are confident, they will relax and settle in to your performance. At the very beginning, it helps to go a little slower and louder while the audience tunes in to you. Once they are with you, you can go anywhere. Trust them to do some of the work themselves; they don't need you to spell everything out too clearly, and will enjoy thinking about your performance if it leaves a few things to the imagination.

OLD
TESTAMENT

Mrs Adam

I had planned to steer clear of the women in the Bible who already have a 'reputation', and focus on the lesser known, but I couldn't really avoid Eve. She is the natural place to begin. The first man and woman in the Bible, whether real or symbolic, are a crucial part of the biblical narrative. Adam names his wife 'Chava' *– in English, Eve. The Hebrew means 'living' or 'life', and we're told he chose it because she is 'the mother of all the living'[1]* Chava *can also be translated as 'stomach', which is interesting, not only in relation to childbirth, but because the feelings, emotions and decisions that make us human seem to live in our core, more often called our guts.*

Mrs Adam has had a difficult time in history with her reputation for taking the forbidden fruit and causing 'the fall of man'. It may be worth noting that 'she also gave some to her husband, who was with her, *and he ate . . .'[2] Adam was right by her side at the time, and should be remembered as equally culpable.*

Banished from the garden where God is their constant companion and life is good, fruitful and eternal, their task is to live up to their original commission of filling and stewarding the earth, but in a more hostile environment, where God is harder to find and death is a real enemy. After their exile, we don't hear much more about this couple other than that they initially have three sons and more children later (the ninth generation producing Noah).

As they are exiled, God speaks in turn to the serpent (Satan), to Eve and to Adam about the consequences of their actions. He warns the snake, 'I will put enmity between you and the woman, and between your offspring and hers . . .'[3] Many commentaries talk of a messianic promise in these verses, subtly revealing God's plan for someone born of a woman to conquer the forces of evil. To the woman he says, 'I will greatly increase your pangs in childbearing; in pain you shall bring forth children . . .'[4] The word 'pain' denotes more than just labour. Birth is only the beginning of the mothering process. 'Bringing forth' children is a much more complex and ongoing task than delivering them.

It is fun to imagine Adam and Eve having experiences for which, as the first people to exist, they had no frame of reference. They had been commissioned by God, 'Be fruitful and multiply',[5] but the first baby, and the way he was delivered, may have been something of a shock. In the hours following the birth, Eve is likely to be on an emotional rollercoaster. You can play that up as much as you like. She could still be in bed, and may be holding the newborn. She's physically exhausted but still elated, and her mind is working overtime to figure things out. I've also played on the idea that women are more instinctive talkers and communicators, giving Eve great pleasure in the use of words.In this piece she may well be having a conversation with God himself.

NOTES

[1]   Genesis 3:20.
[2]   Genesis 3:6, emphasis added.
[3]   Genesis 3:15.
[4]   Genesis 3:16.
[5]   Genesis 1:28.

My God, what was that all about? It hurt like hell. If that's giving birth, why do I feel like death? And it's my job. I can't say I'm delighted. Adam passed out, and he was only watching. He's still down. Snoring.

'Get busy and multiply.' What a palaver. The first stage is fun, I grant you. But this! It wasn't as dignified as I'd hoped. Adam and I have never had secrets from each other, but this was a new level of intimacy. It felt akin to violation. I thought I was going to split open and die. Which was tempting as a get-out, believe me. I got so furious that I couldn't overrule my instinct to live. I was shouting at Adam to put me out of my misery. Somehow, my body knew it had to keep pushing. The elation, when the baby was out! I still feel giddy with the intensity of it. Who cares if it was euphoria or delirium, it felt good. Delirium! That's a good word, isn't it?

Adam asked me, 'Are you still uncomfortable?' I wanted to laugh but I thought my insides might fall out. I *was* warned about the pain. We earned it. I guess my body will heal. But it goes beyond that. It hurts me some-where inside when he cries. He bites when he's feeding, and pulls my hair. I mean the baby, not Adam. Although Adam's not immune from giving me grief either. We argued when he blathered something about postnatal depression.

The first time I saw Adam, he was asleep. Nothing changes! I waited until he opened his eyes and it was

. . . magical. I understood his face. When we discovered we could communicate verbally as well, I almost lost control of my bladder. (I think that's something I might have to get used to now.) Each day was more exquisite than the last. Finding new things to say and do. Even when it took us ages to agree over something, which was most of the time, we savoured every second. Pure heavenliness.

Not now. The best word is 'bereft'. We've lost contact with all that's divine. I hope we can find our way back, somehow. I think the key might be in this 'multiplication'.

Oh no. Maths may not be my strong point, but I've just worked something out. If that damned snake is going to breed, then I'm going to have to produce an army, to give us a fighting chance. Which means doing this all over again. And again and again. Good grief.

I wanted to know, and now I *do* know – I wish I didn't know what I know now. That all joy from hereon will be tempered with pain. Just like childbirth.

(She begins to cry).

Oh, this is ridiculous! I'm like a one-woman water fountain. I was trying to explain to Adam how I really feel, and he looked terrified. I'm hardly surprised, because in the same breath I'd blown my nose, cried, said how much I loved him, snorted, hiccupped and told him I hated him.

He took a deep breath, looked at me full on and started talking. '*Chava*, my life. There is you, there is me, there's our baby. There's the earth, there's growth and promise. There's a future, and we must do what we were made to do, what we've been asked to do. We're here. And life starts here.'

Where on earth did he get that speech from? Childbirth must be more complicated than I thought; *his* hormones must be affected too. He was crying. It would be useful if one of us could hold it together at some point.

We chose this, and we will have to live with it. But there is comfort in the fact that we can reproduce. It gives me hope. We're a work in progress. I've learnt a lot, even today, from what a complete mess I've made. I'll know to put some towels down on the bed next time.

Mrs Cain

The first two sons of Adam and Eve, the brothers Cain and Abel, are notorious as humanity's first recorded murderer and his victim. The seed of the brutal crime appears to have been planted at the moment when '. . . the LORD had regard for Abel and his offering, but for Cain and his offering he had no regard.'[1] A simple fraternal jealousy prompted by what appears to be God's whim. The New Testament explains a bit more. 'By faith Abel offered to God a more acceptable sacrifice than Cain's. Through this he received approval as righteous.'[2] It is not Abel's offering itself that particularly pleases God, it's his faith and devotion. Love is the motive for giving 'the firstlings of his flock, their fat portions.'[3]

Cain gives an offering, too (how generous we don't know) – but his is a mere ritual to placate God and earn his approval. Again, in the New Testament, one of John's letters confirms, 'And why did [Cain] murder him? Because his own deeds were evil and his brother's righteous.'[4] Interestingly, this verse is parcelled up in an exhortation to love one another because 'Whoever does not love abides in death.'[5] Cain's bitter resentment of his brother and the evil intent that would lead to murder began long before the incident with the offerings. This is the reason God responds to them as he does.

However, God gives Cain a chance. Redemption is still possible, but not if he continues with his current behaviour: ' . . .

sin is lurking at the door; its desire is for you, but you must master it.'[6] *Cain doesn't manage to control his anger or hatred. His punishment is to live as a fugitive, far from his land and any sense of the presence of God. He settles 'in the land of Nod', which translates as 'wandering'. Immediately afterwards, he 'knows' his wife and bears a son.*[7] *There is no mention of his wife earlier than this, so I have decided – for artistic, not theological or historical reasons – that he met her after his flight.*

This is a woman battling with her husband's unknown past, and the effect it has on her marriage. She is thoughtful, spending time considering life's meaning, and working things out. Cain is a mystery to be solved, despite the underlying threat of danger he poses. She will not name or admit what he's done, and blames herself for the physical result of his anger and bitterness.

NOTES

[1] Genesis 4:4,5.
[2] Hebrews 11:4, emphasis added.
[3] Genesis 4:4.
[4] 1 John 3:12.
[5] 1 John 3:14.
[6] Genesis 4:7.
[7] Genesis 4:17.

Cain is not a man who loves. He's a man who strives. It doesn't make for romance. He has no sense of the transcendent. He lives with his hands in the ground and this fearsome grip on the belongings, the buildings, the things and the stuff. He works at his own ability to master it, to make it his. His faith is in himself.

I can't call him handsome, though he might have been once. At the corners of his eyes and his mouth there's a downward pull. It gives him a grim look of disappointment, like a gathering storm. He's not a man who talks about . . . anything.

He's restless when he sleeps, thrashing about. He mutters, but all I can make out is 'east of Eden.' I've wondered if that's where he came from. He turned up here in Nod one day and never mentioned family or past, and I couldn't broach the subject. His temper makes me wary. I wanted to know him.

Why is it, when there's a cut in your mouth, you can't help but poke it and irritate it with your tongue? Or you've an ache in a joint, and you keep moving it to feel the pain. Or the uncontrollable urge to squeeze a spot or scratch a sore or pick a scab. I want to scrape off his surface and see what's festering.

So I started to jab him. Prodding away a little harder every day, looking for the bits that sting. And I didn't mind if he exploded because I wanted to see, I wanted to know. I poked until he was raw. Where did you come from? Why did you come here? Who did you leave behind? Why are you so discontented? Why does it drive you? What are you trying to prove? Who are you trying to please? The first crack made my ears ring. 'Why do you insist on pressing me? Do you want to end up like Abel?' My face must've said it, because before a question was on my lips, he carried on, 'What? Who? No one, I don't know, I didn't . . .'

'Who's Abel?'

The second crack almost broke my jaw. It spilled out of him. 'It was their fault, my mother with her stories of Eden and my father endlessly egging her on. Both full of grave warnings. I hated them for it, and I hated the land because I was cheated. I deserved better. So I gave my self-right-eous brother what was coming to him, and got sent from the earth that I'd fought for while he slept in it.' No rain followed the thunder. I don't think he knows how to cry.

The joy in our life is Enoch. In our son, we agree we've made something good. We named the city after him. The city Cain has built with blood and sweat, fighting the land to tame it. Enoch means 'dedicated'. Dedicated to what? To spreading the kingdom of man where people master the stuff but not themselves.

I wanted to know. Now I'm wondering how my hand can keep stroking his brow, soothing him. While my heart is numb, my body aches and I feel sick beyond my stomach. I lie every night next to a : . . . This man I love, who shares my life has . . . And I will serve the sentence. Because I wanted to know.

Mrs Noah

The first draft of Mrs Noah was produced one rainy afternoon, years ago. I'm particularly fond of her because she set this whole project in motion, and because ultimately, right in the early chapters of the Bible,[1] she finds hope in the faithfulness of God. In order to do so, she's dragged onto a floating zoo and, probably – like most women! – ended up doing the lion's share of the work. I wonder how much she laughed in comparison to how often her sense of humour failed her. We never hear how she reacted. I imagine she struggled – and perhaps, when the work was done, when she had played her part in history and had seen the rainbow, she was changed.

At the point we meet her, she feels exhausted, frustrated and put-upon – as any woman in her situation might. Her experience hasn't sapped her strength. If anything, the hard work has made her all the feistier. Her irritation builds and builds until the moment of revelation that makes it all seem worthwhile and renews her resolve to continue.

In her conversation with Noah, he speaks in the spaces between lines, and she listens and responds accordingly. She may be wearing rubber gloves.

NOTE

[1]   Genesis 6 – 9.

Things have come to a head. You know when you reach that moment, and you think: up until now I've grumbled but I've done it, but this is a turning point. And it had better be a complete U-turn. I like to think of myself as a competent woman. I like to think I'm a reasonable woman. I'm happy to do what every woman does in her own home – rule the roost. Only in my case, it's not just a roost. It's a fully stocked zoo. I know what you're thinking, a lot of homes can be a bit zoo-like, especially at feeding time. But mine actually is. You see, this God that my husband thinks is the bee's knees has commissioned us to save the entire animal kingdom from extinction. And the straw that broke this camel's back was that today . . . I've run out of ideas for the catering. I need a holiday. Or at least a long soak in the bath. Just jump in, he says, I'll fish you out later. I could wring his neck. Last time I quizzed my husband about how long it'll take to make sure every last human has drowned, he gave me the 'God's timing' routine. Well, I am sick of waiting. We're having it out.

(She approaches and addresses Noah).

Noah. A word. A word please, Noah. Stop talking to the vines and look at me. I swear you have more to say to those vines than to your own wife.

I'm sorry. I don't like swearing either, but it's getting more difficult not to by the minute; my head is pounding. The peacocks were squawking all night, the elephants trumpet incessantly and the cockerel joined in at 4 a.m. to herald the dawn. Look at me when I'm talking to you. I'm trying here, Noah!

I'm well aware that you're a man, and even 'a man of the soil', but right now there isn't any soil around. And, quite frankly, if you don't stop crushing those grapes, I'll crush yours.

It's very nice of you to want to make me wine. There's nothing I feel like more than a good whine. But if you're honest, you'll only drink it all yourself anyway.

Well, maybe it was below the belt, but at least you're listening. These vines are a good place to start. They're taking over the whole ark. Only yesterday Shem's wife tripped and went sailing into the lion enclosure. The hyenas have never laughed harder. Have you had a word with God yet? You promised me you would. And I think you should talk to Ham about taunting the animals. I don't like his attitude.

He's your son, he *is* your responsibility. You let him get away with everything. That boy takes liberties. And Japheth thought it was funny to teach the parrots to wolf whistle every time I walk past, and make the dogs bark the tune for the Sabbath blessing.

He might well be amusing himself, but it doesn't amuse anybody else. Added to which, one of the camels has just been sick all over the monkeys, and they're kicking up a stink. I cannot continue to clean up after the entire animal kingdom on a daily basis.

I probably do have Seasonal Adjustment Disorder. It's been raining for months. But I think my severe case of Dysfunctional Husband Disorder is a more serious problem.

What's that you say?

Yes, I can see it's a dove. I've become quite good at distinguishing animals.

So what if it has a branch? Are you listening to me?

A tree?

Well, of course the water level must have gone down a bit, but it's not far enough yet, is it? What, do you want to build a tree house now? Seasickness is bad enough, but vertigo's not much fun either.

I know. We would have died if it weren't for your special warning. But quite frankly, being fathoms under water seems preferable to this right now. I'm staying behind next time God decides to wipe out the human race.

How do you know he won't do it again?

Oh, well, let's hope he's better at keeping his promises than you are. Because you still haven't cut the tigers claws, wormed the sheep, or treated the donkeys' fleas.

I need a promise that someone will do something to sort out this stinking hovel. And I'd rather it didn't involve water.

(She sees something behind Noah).

Noah! Look! The sun's coming out. And there's a . . . a . . . what is it? It's a waterfall of colour. What's it called?

Rainbow.

(Her attention leaves Noah and she addresses her original listener[s]).

Glorious.

Sunshine and rain. Joy and tears. Noah gets it, of course, and smiles to himself that it all worked out. But I really feel God means it for me. I still get a bit nervous when it starts raining, probably always will. But there's the rainbow; I see it and I know. It's like a wink from the Almighty. Right. Mucking out time.

Mrs Abraham

Abraham is the founding father of both the Muslim and Jewish people, the former from his first son, Ishmael, and the latter from his second son, Isaac. His story features in some detail early in the Bible,[1] including the fact that after Sarah's death, he remarried and fathered six more children in his second century, living to the age of 175. The descendants both of Ishmael and Isaac, and of these other children, have fought each other for land from the time of the Bible to the present day.

The biblical narrative moves from Abraham to Isaac, before passing on to his son Jacob, then through the generations to King David and his most famous descendant, Jesus.

Abraham's wife, Sarah, enjoys a close relationship with her husband and, to their joy, after years of being unable to have children, manages to conceive Isaac when she's in her nineties. It is interesting to note how much of a part she plays in the outcome of events. In the days of their infertility, it is her idea that Abraham sleep with her servant, Hagar, and it is because of her that Hagar and Ishmael are sent away when Isaac is weaned. The consequences of her actions will reverberate through the centuries. Is this banishment simply an indication of an insecure woman, resorting yet again to manipulation to get what she wants? Or has she been maligned by history? Might there be another reason for Sarah's actions?

The book of Genesis recounts that Sarah saw the son of Hagar the Egyptian tsachaq *her son Isaac.*[2] *The Hebrew word* tsachaq *is translated differently in various versions as to laugh, mock or play with, or even to jest, toy or sport with. The New Testament says, '. . . the child who was born according to the flesh [Ishmael]* dioko *the child who was born according to the Spirit [Isaac]'.*[3] *Here the Greek word* dioko *can be translated 'persecute, trouble, molest or harass'. It's a fleeting mention, but bullying seems to be the issue. How does any mother deal with that? Sarah's actions may have repercussions for history, but she's a mother trying to do the best for her child in a dysfunctional family situation. Despite the mess, God says he plans to multiply this family across the entire globe, making them a blessing to the world.*

Although she is elderly, being a mother has reinvigorated Sarah. She is sprightly, talkative, and has a sharp sense of humour and a twinkle in her eye. She is delighted to be at her first parents' evening, and eager to hear about her son's progress. I don't think it's necessary to play the part 'old'. Although some comedy would come from representing her age, in performance it will be more helpful to think instead about the impact on her character of her extraordinary life.

NOTES

[1] Genesis 11:27 – 25:18.
[2] Genesis 21:9.
[3] Galatians 4:29.

(Sarah arrives and takes a seat).

Is it Mrs Ellison? Wonderful. I'm here for Isaac. No, I'm not his grandmother. No, I'm not his great-grand-mother. I'm sure we haven't got time for twenty questions, so let's speed this up: I'm his mother. Yes, it is a bit of a shocker, isn't it? I'm well aware that I'm a wrinkled old bat, especially for my first parents' evening, but you should see his father! He moves quite fast with a Zimmer frame.

Don't bother stuffing a hanky in your mouth, have a good laugh instead. We do, whenever we see ourselves in a mirror. That's why we called our son Isaac. It means 'laughter'. Hilarious! Imagine me getting pregnant at 90. No, I realize you'd probably rather not.

After seventy years of desperation, I can't begin to tell you . . . You feel like a mockery of womanhood. Serving a life sentence of longing for the one thing you can't make happen – even if you stand on your head for six hours every time you have sex. Then your useless bits shrivel up anyway and it's too late.

Over the years, Abraham – Abe, yes. Yes, he does have another son. Ishmael. Did you teach him, too? Right. Well, it's complicated. You see . . . Where to start . . .

Abe has had a close acquaintance with a god he calls 'the Lord', who talks to him about all the big whys and wherefores and what-to-dos. This god, the Lord, told my Abe he would be the father of a multitude of nations. Well, it's an honour, isn't it? And I was clearly getting in the way, with my useless body. Abe told me he'd love me come what may, and was assured the Lord could fulfil his plans. But I wasn't on familiar terms with the Lord. Not then. So, how could I trust what he promised?

So I pre-empted him. It's only natural to take matters into your own hands, isn't it? I suggested Abe sleep with my help around the house, Hagar. Egyptian girl, pretty. He said he wasn't sure that was what the Lord had in mind, but a man's a man when all's said and done. He took one look at her in her negligee and followed her like a lamb. He barely had to lay his pyjamas on her bed and she got pregnant. That was Ishmael. What a disaster that turned out to be. Oh, I don't mean the child, it's not his fault. I mean of my own making. Hindsight. Easy now I have a son of my own who's turning five. I'm longing to hear all about Isaac's progress. You don't want to hear any more about me. Oh, you do? Well, I suppose it is a tad intriguing.

Abe was pottering around his trees one day as usual – slowly, when three men turned up without warning. Abe loves company and insisted they stay for dinner. He chivvied me into action, a slap-up meal as quick as fast food. Now I know I shouldn't listen at keyholes. I only wanted to know how the grub was going down. But I couldn't help hearing one of them ask where I was, and then tell Abe that this time next year I would have a child. Laugh? I nearly died trying to hold it in. If my face is shrivelled as an old prune, imagine what my uterus looks like! Added to which, I didn't know if Abe would manage it. At our age, would pleasure even be possible? I'd gone off that kind of thing since the menopause.

I had no idea who the three men were. I figured they must have escaped from the local locked unit. When I went in to put seconds in front of them, one of them asked, 'Why did you laugh?' I tried to look incredulous, and innocent, and smother the hysteria. But then I caught Abe's eye, and let out this dirty great snigger. He had a 'trust-her-to-let-me-down' look all over his face. The man responded, 'Is anything impossible for the Lord?' I shrieked, 'But swapping incontinence pads for nipple pads – you have to admit it's funny.' They evidently didn't think so.

How could I believe such a thing? And that kind of hope is cruel. But Abe was convinced. He got to his duties with renewed fervour. Sorry – too much information. Anyway, he was right. It worked and here I am. Living proof that nothing is too difficult for the Lord, as our visitor said. Tell me, please, is anything to difficult for Isaac? Or is he a whiz in the classroom with the inherited wisdom of his ancient parents?

That's good.

Umm, I don't know about Ishmael, I'm afraid, Mrs Ellison. He'll be about 18 by now. Did his mother come and tell you, when she took him out of school, that I'd thrown her out like a jealous harpy? I'm sure she didn't tell you that for a few months I'd been finding marks on Isaac. A few angry red patches at first, followed by bruises, grazes, welts. He'd started to get clingy, a bit tearful and withdrawn. Then I saw him flinch when his brother reached in front of him for bread. I warned Hagar that I suspected Ishmael. The boy was 14, not a child.

What do you do in this school when you suspect an older boy is hurting one of the little ones, Mrs Ellison? What would you do if it were *your* son? I was out of my mind with worry. It's hard enough for Isaac having decrepit parents.

I didn't take any pleasure in banishing them. I didn't know what else to do. Thankfully, Abe says nothing I have done will prevent the fulfilment of God's original promise. Our Isaac's descendants will be like stars in the heavens and sand on the shore. But Ishmael will not be forgotten. Brothers by blood, but divided by destiny.

Do you ever feel, Mrs Ellison, as a teacher, that you might be holding the future of nations in your hands? And do you ever wonder that the smallest action on your part might have the greatest of consequences?

(A pause before she looks up and breaks the moment).

Look, the next mother's here, I'd better go. She doesn't look old enough to reproduce, but what would I know. I'll come in again; I'd love to see some of Isaac's work. If he's anything like his father, he'll be going down in history.

Mrs Jacob (1 and 2)

Jacob, son of Isaac, son of Abraham, flees his home to escape his murderous brother whom he has robbed of his birthright – the blessing of the first-born. In the country of his asylum, he marries and becomes the father of twelve sons. God renames him 'Israel', and his sons are the foundation for the exponential growth of the 'Children of Israel' – a new nation of twelve tribes.

When Jacob first escapes to his Uncle Laban's land, he meets and falls in love with his cousin, Rachel, and gives seven years of hard work to earn her hand in marriage. But Laban cheats him, just as Jacob has cheated his brother (the name Jacob means 'deceiver'). On the wedding night, Rachel is replaced by her older sister, Leah, and Jacob chooses to work another seven years to gain his adored Rachel as well. Each sister has a maid, Zilpah and Bilhah, who are dragged into the competition between Leah and Rachel to provide children for Jacob. Rachel does not manage to conceive until ten sons and a daughter have already been produced. She eventually has Joseph (of Technicolour Dreamcoat *fame), then dies giving birth to Benjamin. These two are Jacob's favourites, because of his love for Rachel.*

The bulk of the narrative concerning these two women appears in two chapters in Genesis, in little detail.[1] It is an extraordinary story. The sisters appear to have little choice in their lives, being bought and sold in marriage contracts brokered by their father, and yet they have so much fight. Their competitiveness to reproduce for the man they share goes as far as offering their maids as surrogate mothers. (We don't hear any complaint or intervention from Jacob, who seems quite happy to put his seed wherever it's requested.)

The strength of the conflict is reflected in Rachel's naming of Naphtali, which means 'wrestling'. 'With mighty wrestlings I have wrestled with my sister . . .'[2] It's rooted in the mighty problem of two sisters in love with, and both married to, the same man. Before Jacob came into their lives, they may have been loving and close, but circumstances have now consigned them to a lifetime of pain, hurt and loss.

I wondered if they might come to a point, after many years, when they would like to be reconciled. How would that happen? So many torn relationships remain in tatters because no one knows how to make the first move to resolution. The task of repairing the damage can seem too big to know where to start. Even if reconciliation is longed for, pride and fear can anchor people in their entrenched positions.

Rachel is probably seen as emotional, dramatic and self-centred, making her feelings known. Leah is more practical, and weary, having kept her emotions locked up for so long. Their tragedy is in how similar they are, but because they don't communicate, they never discover they feel the same way.

When putting this on stage, choose where to place Leah and Rachel. They may be sitting close together but facing away from each other. They could be apart, facing in the same direction. You might want them to face each other across a room. It will depend on the performance space, and on how you want to represent the relationship. The placement of actors can communicate extra layers of meaning.

NOTES

1. Genesis 29:1 – 30:24.
2. Genesis 30:8.

LEAH:

It's one thing suspecting your husband has another woman. It's another knowing it. And it's another still, knowing it's your sister. I thought I could make him love me, but he has always loved, and will always love, her. The beautiful one, the graceful one, the younger and thinner model.

RACHEL:

I used to love my sister. As girls, we shared everything. Games, gifts, every dream and secret. We shared a bed. I never thought we'd share a husband. We can't be comrades, we're set face to face instead of side by side. He may say he doesn't love her, but it doesn't stop him going to her, does it? Because she's the fertile one. The reproduction machine who just has to think of falling pregnant, and she does.

LEAH:

People wonder if I consented to the switch. When Rachel came home saying she'd been to the well and met our cousin, arrived from out west, my heart leapt. We'd heard of the two sons of our aunt. Strong and determined, and apparently handsome. I wasn't disappointed; he was articulate and solid. And I wanted him.

RACHEL:

I was praying Leah would find someone to marry. I knew Daddy would want her seen to before me. But Jacob was mine. I loved him from the first day I clapped eyes on him. So attentive and earnest. In the seven years he toiled for me, we planned and whispered and dreamt of the night we'd be allowed to stay together. Seven years. Until Daddy put my dress on her and sent her into the ceremony, while I wept in the chicken coop. Jacob was furious; I've never seen him beside himself like that. But what could he do? He promised another seven years for me, his only intention.

LEAH:
For a week, he was just mine. The first night was rapturous. The next few days were half-hearted, once he knew it was me. And then she was there, too. Why did he get to have her, paid as an advance?

RACHEL:
I had waited and dreamed and longed for that moment and, when I got there, his bed had her smell. For the first time, I wished her harm. It wasn't her fault, but that didn't matter. She was in my place, and two people cannot live one dream.

LEAH:
Over so many years, we've fallen into a sort of routine. Although there is occasional calm, there's never peace.

RACHEL:
We're trapped in this agonizingly slow game, played with child pawns. And I've borrowed two, but none of the pieces are really mine.

LEAH:
Now Rachel's storms are raging again, because I'm pregnant. Four sons in quick succession, then two more, plus this bump. A gift from God to prove my worthiness as a wife. To buy Jacob's love by admiration. Rachel got so desperate she used her maid as a surrogate womb to mother two boys. She uses them to wound me.

RACHEL:
The second is called Naphtali, 'my wrestling'. He's a bruiser. I wanted to win a point. Leah couldn't handle the slowing of her incubator body; the one thing that makes her feel adequate. So she fought back the same way, and had two sons by her maid. But then she popped out a couple more of her own, and is fat with another already. It's sickening.

I just want to carry a child, inside, to know that I can make it grow. I've seen countless delivered now, but never from my own useless womb. Jacob holds me and wipes away my tears, and hates to see me desolate. But he doesn't know what to say. And the hours he spends gazing into my eyes are stolen when his body answers its call with her, the functioning one.

LEAH:
She need not fight. She's his favourite. And I am tired. I've begun to pray that she will conceive. I have waived my rights to him. I cannot go on bearing her pain.

RACHEL:
I made him stay with me last week, all week. If I failed again, my emptiness would be my fault alone. I was sick this morning. I feel slightly odd. There's a burning sensation in the base of my spine. But I don't feel I've won anything.

LEAH:
I have surrendered. We've played games for too long with no winner. And I would like to be on the same side.

RACHEL:
I thought I would want to wave it in her face and stamp a victory dance and kick up a fuss as always. But I can't. I don't wish her defeat. And I don't know how to tell her.

LEAH:
We're so different now.

RACHEL:
We're so different now.

LEAH:
If I told her, I don't think she'd understand.

RACHEL:
She wouldn't understand.

LEAH:
And so things will go on as they have.

RACHEL:
Things will go on.

Mrs Potiphar

When friends asked what I was writing, a number said, 'So you'll be doing Mrs Potiphar, then.' She was far from the first to come to my mind, but she has obviously struck a chord as a biblical wife of interest, possibly with those who like a little sexual frisson in their stories! The success of the musical Joseph and the Technicolour Dreamcoat *probably hasn't done her PR any harm. The narrative in Genesis 39 is rich in plot, generous in detail, and contemporary in its portrayal of human nature.*

Mrs Potiphar was possibly a trophy wife, lonely and bored, who found herself physically attracted to Joseph. After all, he was 'handsome and good-looking.'[1] I think her head was also turned by his success and confidence – looks and power are an irresistible combination. Blend infatuation with the arrogance of a woman who could have everything she wanted whenever she wanted it, and you have a fairly potent recipe for disaster.

As a red-blooded young man, how did Joseph manage to resist such persistent advances from his boss's wife for so long? Perhaps it has something to do with the repetition at the beginning and end of the passage that 'the LORD was with Joseph.'[2] Pitted against her status, Joseph finds himself in prison, with no chance to speak in his own defence.[3] Here is a perfect example of the eighteenth-century William Congreve quote, 'Hell hath no fury like a woman scorned.' This one certainly wreaked her revenge on the man who had rejected her advances and dented her pride.

She may be filing her nails, or eating grapes.

NOTES

[1] Genesis 39:6.
[2] Genesis 39:2,3,21,23.
[3] Genesis 39:19,20.

I still have his coat. He is languishing in an Egyptian jail. Without a coat. If I have anything to do with it, he will remain at Pharaoh's pleasure until his handsome face has creased and faded grey. No one makes a fool of me. Lessons must be learnt. I will not be crossed. I'm not married to the captain of the guard for nothing; I mean, come on, there have to be some perks to a lifetime with Potiphar.

Have you ever met a man who can do no wrong? Yes, I know *all* men *think* they can do no wrong, and Potiphar blusters with the best of them, but Joseph was different. He had something I couldn't put my finger on . . . and believe me, I wanted to put my hands all over it.

I was so close. I'd been working on him for weeks. Impressive control, I thought, but beginning to find his coolness completely infuriating. So I hurried things along, dismissed the servants and followed him into the parlour. We were alone. Potiphar was off doing whatever frightfully boring things he does all day. I was Nile-bathed and looking luscious. I'm not embarrassed to say it; there's never been a man who's refused me – especially when I'm laced with Eau de Sphinx. He gave me the usual 'I couldn't do it to your husband' and 'I value my job' routine. Knowing I'm married to Potiphar does seem to strike fear into the younger ones. It doesn't strike anything into me. Dull. I didn't think Joseph would last long if I added more visible flesh into the equation; the flesh of a five-times straight Miss Nile winner. But none of my usually failsafe techniques breached the resistance. The young man went on protesting. The most convincing performance I've ever seen.

His line was: 'How could I sin against God?' I've never heard that one before. What does a god have to do with anything? But I could see that for him, it did. It had everything to do with it, everything to do with everything. Our raft of gods was nothing to him, and Potiphar wasn't much more, but the Hebrew God was his master.

There's nothing wrong with Joseph. No little performance problem. No excuses. He's as red-blooded as the next man, I can tell. But somehow, there's a different power at work in him. Finally, I went in for an embarrassing last-ditch attempt to grab him; having seen his naked faith, I wanted even more to have his naked flesh. He was gone so fast I almost saw his smoke. The northern whippet had shot out of his coat.

I had to think on my feet. With his coat in my hand and my face flushed red, I was hardly a picture of innocence. He had kept his honour, but where was mine? So I screamed assault and performed a blinder and was so incensed I believed it myself.

But there's some kind of . . . *reality* I can't shake from my memory: his simple assurance of God. Something's left the house now Joseph's gone. There's a missing presence, bigger than the space he occupied. My sources tell me that mysterious favour has followed him to prison. We've lost our Hebrew with his God in tow and I miss them.

I still have his coat.

Mrs Pharaoh

The Exodus was a triumph for the children of Israel, a victory over their oppressors, remembered every year by the Jewish people, to this day. The story is recounted in the book of Exodus, and referred to in many other parts of the Bible with joy and thanksgiving.

Yet the uneasy truth is that in any battle there are winners and losers, and there are casualties on both sides. For the Egyptian people, Pharaoh's determination not to let the Hebrews go incurs a profusion of ever-more disastrous plagues, culminating in the death of every first-born son – including his own.[1] Even though the Hebrews were subject to intense suffering at the hands of the Egyptians, it's difficult to understand a God who 'allows' or even 'instigates' this type of punishment. He tells Moses to say to Pharaoh, 'Thus says the LORD: "Israel is my firstborn son. I said to you, 'Let my son go that he may worship me.' But you refused to let him go; now I will kill your firstborn son."'[2] This makes for very uncomfortable reading. Some scholars explain that societies like the Egypt of that time, which choose to ignore the lifestyle and values of a monotheistic faith, end up bringing destruction on themselves. Others argue that Israel was so crucial to God's ultimate plan to redeem the whole world that he has to go to extreme lengths to ensure their survival.[3] Either way, it's one for discussion.

The Bible asks more questions than it answers, and challenges us to wrestle with cosmic problems. No matter how difficult aspects of this story may be, the Exodus is a large and important part of the biblical narrative, and I have confronted the challenge head on by telling it from this unusual perspective.

The bond between a parent and a child is unlike any other, and surely Pharaoh's wife would feel the loss of her son as much as any mother. She might also begin to be able to relate to God as another suffering parent: he feels the loss of his children here in Egypt and later, in the New Testament, will feel the loss of his own Son, Jesus. Pharaoh's wife may well have been angry with God and within her rights to voice her complaint, but I have chosen instead to allow her to connect with him for the first time.

She is the cool, collected wife of the highest-ranking statesman. She is also a grieving mother. In her devastation she is in a trance-like state, at the stage of grief where she feels so numb that she is almost outside herself, looking down on her own plight and able to comment on it with insight. There are moments when anger bursts through, heavy with blame for her dead husband, whom she believes is responsible for her loss.

NOTES

[1] Exodus 11:1–6; 12:29–32.
[2] Exodus 4:22.
[3] Thanks to Graham Tomlin, Dean of St Mellitus College, for these and other insights.

I warned him. I told him, 'This is no time for power games! This is an opponent like never before. Walk away, let the damn slaves go! It will show you're a bigger man in the end.' It's his fault. I thought the frogs were a good one. I laughed. Amphibians are a relief after a week assaulted by the stench of stale blood. These Hebrews and their God are certainly creative. Frogs! Ribbiting hilarious. Until they made a carpet so thick that walking was a mission even for the least squeamish, and they were piled up dead in rotting heaps.

Gnats. Flies. Swarming so viciously that breathing was a challenge. Animals all dead, so we've no meat or milk. Then boils, festering all over, oozing pus and pain. Our best magicians, long since out-magicked, were nursing their pride as much as their putrefied skin.

And still my stubborn husband wouldn't shift. Proving himself unmovable. Even cracking the whip to show himself boss.

So it continued. A bit of bad weather doesn't bother Egyptians; we can handle storms even if we are nursing left-over boils in painful places. But this was unearthly. Hail and fire from the sky lashed every last shelter and tree to the ground. People died, and no one could get out to pull them back indoors . . . While my petulant husband threw tantrums like a toddler and I implored him for mercy.

He would soften to my pleading and agree with me, 'Enough is enough.' Until the situation eased, and somehow he'd be fully resolved again to stand firm on what he knew to be his. Or the tattered remains of it.

His father was right. The Hebrews were increasing too fast and growing too strong. Something needed to be done. It was self-preservation. So the plan was made. But this one was saved. This thorn in our side. The baby pulled out of the water. Named by my husband's sister. Raised alongside them. Disappeared, fugitive, for forty years, and back now with reinforcements: his mouthy brother and this God of theirs.

Is this their vengeance? Egypt is ruined. It was ruined even before the locusts came. I had thought there was nothing more to take, but the buzzing black clouds stripped the place clean as a bone. The darkness may have spared us the sight of our skeletal land, but it held us hostage for three unmoving days, and I felt it would quench the very air from my lungs as it pressed in, heavy. Why must his heart be so hard? My husband, the bulwark. Made to defend, but retaining more suffering than he's keeping out. Why couldn't he climb down? He said it more than once. I heard him, pillar-hidden and hardly daring to breathe. I was surprised; he seemed somehow more human for the words that were strangely new in his mouth: 'Forgive me. I've wronged the Lord your God and wronged you. Of course you must go.' And I felt weak with relief. But then he would turn like the unstoppable twice-a-day tide and deny they should leave unless over his dead and self-righteous body.

And death it was. Not him, but worse. My son. My son. My beautiful son. Long-limbed, dark-skinned, sweet-natured and temperate, so unlike his father. Grown to a man, but still young and elastic. Now never to age. Because of his father's unshakeable pride. I hate him for it. It is his fault. In his momentary pain, which I think he felt more like an insult than grief, he relented. Gave them a head start, said that was it. But he couldn't. He couldn't admit this God was bigger than him, or that anyone in heaven or earth had more power. And he gave chase. Took his whole army. I heard his fading shouts, 'We've got them now! They'll be trapped at the coast! Payback time, boys!'

His death is too small a payment for my son. And I believe the God of the Hebrews knows my pain. His plagues were a parent-to-parent plea.

I know what it is to love a child, a fierce love. I would kill to protect him, take life to make sure of his. I understand love, protection, salvation at all costs. I understand. I have learned, as Pharaoh would not. And now never shall.

After all he'd seen, how could he think he was in with a chance? The God that rules every element, and has the very power of life and death, could have no problem with the sea. None of us saw it from here, but rumour is, it parted. And the Hebrews walked over, safe and bemused, until the final step of the final child, and the water rushed back . . . Pharaoh and his choiceless army under it.

Mrs Joshua

Joshua is one of my all-time favourite Bible superstars. He is present and active in a huge (and exciting) portion of the early history of the Jewish people.

It was in the process of looking through the narrative of his lifespan and deciding which particular moment was the focal point, that I realized how tirelessly he must have worked. He is first an assistant to Moses,[1] serving the children of Israel day in, day out, a general factotum, spy[2] and soldier.[3] Later, he becomes Moses' successor,[4] leading the people, acting as their judge, their guide and their army General. He defeats town after town (of which Jericho is the first and most famous),[5] city after city, and just when he's due for a comfortable retirement, he turns lawyer and oversees the division of the conquered land between the twelve tribes.[6]

We're told he lived for 110 years,[7] during which time no bad word is said of him. He is the quintessential hero – talented, dedicated, successful, and morally perfect to boot. Did he have any faults at all? Perhaps this is why I find him so attractive!

But his very dedication to duty raises a question. Did this man ever rest? Or was he a workaholic? When someone is working flat out 'for God', how easy is it to find an appropriate work/life balance? If Joshua struggled with this, his wife would no doubt have had something to say about it.

In this piece, she is a completely normal, natural and down-to-earth woman, the kind we all know and are now. She juggles family and home, public duties and trips to the supermarket. She is the contemporary voice of Mrs Ordinary, a direct foil to a man who, historically, is Mr Extraordinary.

She approaches Joshua in his study. He is surrounded by papers. She may well be carrying a notebook and pen with her collected research. He is also involved in the conversation; his comments are not heard by us, but she is responding to them.

NOTES

[1] See Exodus, Numbers and Deuteronomy.
[2] Numbers 13.
[3] Exodus 17.
[4] Deuteronomy 31.
[5] Joshua 6.
[6] Joshua 13 onwards.
[7] Joshua 24:29.

Joshua, sweet pea – what?

Why don't you like sweet pea?

What do you want me to call you? Stud muffin? Is that manly enough? Oh, don't be silly, there's no mistaking your testosterone. Ever since you started traipsing up and down Sinai with Moses and a pile of stone tablets all those years ago, your biceps have been busting out of your T-shirt.

Of course I'm not complaining. I'm honoured to have a husband who's so . . . well-packaged. Even if it does make me feel inadequate.

Thank you for saying so, but after the children I'm under no illusions. Can I get to the point of why I came in? There's been talk of a new Top Trumps 'All-Star Warriors'. I'm submitting your details. Quit with the humility, of course you'll be in. Your card will be the one kids squabble over. This is what I've got so far:

(She refers to her notebook).

Nationality: Israel, tribe of Ephraim.

Rank: Top Dog. I know that's not a rank, but 'Leader' just doesn't have enough gusto. 'General' is too vague and 'Field Marshal' sounds like some kind of sports' day attendant. So Top Dog'll have to do. Unless you prefer Top Gun.

I don't know what a gun is, but it sounds good, doesn't it?

OK, 'Leader' it is, but I don't think it does you justice.

Battles fought: 49.

Well, it's an educated guess, really; you've defeated thirty-one kings, but there've been more battles than that. They all roll into one as far as I'm concerned.

Battles won: 48.

I know. I've put that the one you lost wasn't your fault and you won it the second time round, once you'd sorted Achan out, the sneaky little cheater.

No, I haven't put 'sneaky little cheater'.

Miracle involvement: Most notably the day when, at your request, the sun stood still in the sky for a whole day until the Amorites were defeated. Also, Jericho's walls collapsing without you even touching them. And the stopping of the River Jordan as Israel walked over. It may not be as big as the Red Sea, but it's still impressive.

I know it was God that did it, but it doesn't say 'miracles performed', it's 'miracle involvement'. And whoever *did it* you were *there*. Anyway, seems to me God does miracles more often when *you're* around than the rest of us.

I know you two are close. I'm not grumbling, we all get the benefits.

Right, what shall I put for special weapon?

Don't be daft – I can't put the Holy Spirit. Well, for one thing, he's not a weapon!

I see your point. If it means the secret of your success, then that is the answer, isn't it? Tough one. Well, we'll put it down and see what they say.

Most quoted saying: Your favourite is 'Always be bold and courageous', but those are God's words really, not yours. So, if it has to be original, we should go for: 'As for me and mine, we'll serve the Lord.' It's not as warrior-like, but it *is* your motto.

Physical flaws: None that I've noticed.

You haven't! You knocked me off my feet all those years ago with one sweep of your eyelashes, and you've still got it. I've told you before, if the kids get your looks and your character, they'll be laughing.

From me? Umm . . . well, they should inherit my good taste.

OK, last one. Character defects: Workaholic.

It is fair, Joshua! You don't even know what a work/life balance is. You're so rarely here. You're more married to your work than you are to me.

I know God is always with me, and that's all very well, but sometimes I'd rather you were with me. I know. I know it's not just a job. I know how much it means to you. I'm just saying.

You don't come bounding home from battle like you used to. Maybe you could think about retirement soon.

I disagree. I think retiring would be incredibly coura- geous – who knows what Israel would get up to without you?

You may well rest when you're buried in your own plot, but wouldn't it be nice to enjoy it first? I can see you're going to be just as busy as a property lawyer as a fight- ing machine. Look at those piles of paperwork! Your biceps will still be called into action.

Well, thanks a lot for belittling the home front. I can tell you, Mr Always-Be-Bold-and-Courageous, life here has an air of the battlefield about it most days. Never mind the kitchen packed with warring children, I'm forever defending myself against killing looks from other women. The other day, I got sick of it and shouted at someone in the supermarket, 'It's not like Jericho at home, you know. He doesn't march around the bedroom seven times and sound the trumpets till my clothes fall off!' No, he leaves his experimental warfare for the enemy, and comes home to pass out on the sofa with his mouth open.

(She has a change of heart, and smiles).

But catching flies or not, he's a fine specimen. And he's *my* fine specimen. My Top Trump. No, it's not a comment about your digestive problems. Come on, leave the paperwork, let's go to bed early for once. Show me you're as bold and courageous when you're here with me as when you're away fighting for me.

I don't need a hero. I need a husband.

Mrs David, HRH

As the Ark of the Covenant arrives in Jerusalem, King David, surrounded by priests, musicians and singers, 'danced before the LORD with all his might'.[1] We're told that while he did so he was 'girded with a linen ephod.'[2] During the rest of the celebrations we're told he was wearing 'a robe of fine linen.'[3] He had removed his royal outer garments and was dressed in a simple tunic. Perhaps this had some deep spiritual significance, or maybe he just needed to take off the robe to be able to dance unencumbered. If he was dressed in a nightie-like garment, why has it passed into common reference that David danced naked?

It is probably due to the comment of his disgusted wife, Michal, who repeatedly says David has 'shamelessly uncovered'[4] himself. The verb here is galah, which is a tricky one to translate. It has over fifteen different meanings in its Old Testament usage. As well as being used specifically with reference to uncovering nudity, it is also used for general uncovering, variously translated as revealing, appearing, discovering, disclosing, and being open.

We can't know for certain what Michal's objection to David's dance was, but she appears to be mighty put out that her husband was 'showing himself up'. Without his kingly robes, he is as common a man as any other, a completely uninhibited one at that. Interestingly, the ephod is usually the garb of a priest.

David chooses to be dressed as a priest, a servant of the Lord and of the people, rather than as their ruling monarch.

As *the daughter of the previous king (Saul), the first Mrs David may have had fixed ideas about how a king should behave and, in this moment, David clearly falls short of all of them. We're told that she 'despised' him for it.*[5] *'Despising' in the Hebrew here means 'a lack of due respect', and carries its own consequences.*

Michal is probably a good example of how past baggage can breed bitterness. Although she turns it on David, it is she who ultimately bears the damage. She had 'no child to the day of her death.'[6] *Perhaps she became sterile, or perhaps David never wanted to sleep with her again. Or is it a symbolic way of saying that this was a woman who was so critical of others that she became locked into a destructive attitude, unable to uphold or affirm life in any way?*

I was fascinated by her sarcasm (you don't see much of that in the Bible!): 'How the king of Israel honoured himself today',[7] *she mocks. I have incorporated her sarcasm into the piece, but also explored what kind of pain might have been hidden behind this scornful rant. She is not necessarily telling the truth, particularly when she says she is not sorry. Her jealousy of David's joy brings her to a place of desolation that she regrets, even if she won't admit it.*

NOTES

1   2 Samuel 6:14.
2   2 Samuel 6:14.
3   1 Chronicles 15:27.
4   See 2 Samuel 6:20.
5   2 Samuel 6:16.
6   2 Samuel 6:23.
7   2 Samuel 6:20.

He's the best dancer I've ever seen. Seriously. A raw talent with a hidden gift. It's the way each body part moves in complete independence of the others. The way he's immaculately out of time with the music. The way his sweat lands on the spectators. The way he loses his balance with successful regularity. The way he endangers every unfortunate soul who gets too near.

After everything I've done for him, this is how I'm repaid. It was worse than the proverbial dad at a wedding. It was humiliating. Flinging his limbs about. It's a mercy they're well attached.

I used to love him. I was devoted to him. Now, everything he does irritates the hell out of me. I'm the daughter of a king. I'm used to certain standards of behaviour – corruption and murder, and other shows of power. Not idiotic dancing and debasement. Leaping like some demented frog. He abandoned all thoughts of dignity, all thoughts of . . . me.

He forgets I put my neck on the block to save his life. He escaped death thanks to me. Then he was away so long that my father set me up with one of his cronies and, considering I was an abandoned wife, it was my best option. I settled. We were happy in an everyday kind of way. He adored me. But then a few political operations later and David is king. Of course, he had to demand me back at his side as a matter of honour. Poor Paltiel wept and followed me all the way there like a puppy. Pathetic as it was, I preferred it to this.

David's still a boy. 'I don't care,' he shrugged. 'I was dancing for the Lord, and it won't be the last time. It won't even be the worst time. I'll make even more of a fool of myself in my own eyes and yours. But I'll be honoured for it – for putting God first and praising him for what he's done for me and for all Israel.'

Oh well, that's all right, then. That's made you shoot right up in my estimation. You go for it, whenever you want. You just get out there and show them how their king cares not a hoot for his reputation, and your public displays of lunacy shall win my respect for ever. I hate him. I *hate* him. The view from the window was bad enough; I couldn't bear the thought of getting any closer. When we spoke afterwards, I felt my skin crawling.

This must be what it feels like. A hollow emptiness in the pit of me. The end of love. As he walked away, I knew the back of him is all I'll see from now on. I'm not sorry. I've got this permanently running flashback of his face. Eyes closed. Wild grin. And his naked joy.

What has he got to be joyful about? He's a fool. With two left feet.

Mrs Solomon the 364th

The son of David and Bathsheba, Solomon ruled Israel as king for forty prosperous years. We're told that among his wives, whom he 'clung to . . . in love', were 'seven hundred princesses and three hundred concubines'.[1] The majority of them were not Hebrews, and the writer of the book of Kings blames them for eventually turning Solomon's heart away from God to their religions. Nevertheless, because of his promises to his father, David, God continues to bless Solomon, but warns that the kingdom will be split in two during the reign of his son, which is indeed the case.[2]

Solomon was famous for three things. Firstly, the wisdom he had requested from God, and which was granted.[3] He authored many proverbs, and stories were told of his wise judgements.[4] Secondly, he was known for his wealth, building a beautiful temple for God and an opulent palace for himself, prompting the visit of the Queen of Sheba. This wealth was amassed not only from the gifts of those who visited to hear his wisdom, but also by high taxes imposed on his subjects.[5] Thirdly, he is assumed by many to be the author of the Song of Songs, the most romantic and erotic love poetry in the Bible, though some find its message elusive and unclear.

This piece depends not just on the Song of Songs, but also on thoughts from Solomon's diary-like musings in Ecclesiastes that reveal something of his eventual struggles with the short-comings of the life he had created for himself. Despite his wisdom and wealth, he can sound morbidly depressed, until he realizes that it is only God who can give enjoyment of the gifts he has received.[6]

The Bible provides a great deal of information about Solomon's exploits, but almost none about the women with whom he shared them. I have chosen to tell the story of one of the wives who may have grown up knowing who Solomon was. She could still have been quite young when widowed. I've made her the one woman described in the Song of Songs although, of course, those verses could have been collated from poems to any number of his wives, or may not actually have been written by him at all.

As a wife rather than a concubine, she is likely to have been of noble birth and probably a stunning beauty. She was a young innocent and still has romantic notions, but her experience has led her to be more of a realist now. She could be in the palace, looking at the pointless luxury of the surroundings.

NOTES

[1]   1 Kings 11:2,3.
[2]   1 Kings 11:1–13.
[3]   1 Kings 3:3–14.
[4]   1 Kings 3:16–28.
[5]   1 Kings 10.
[6]   Ecclesiastes 2:24–26.

Isn't it odd how, when somebody dies, you say you've lost them? Is it because we don't know where the person goes when the body's done with? I've lost my husband. He died a few days ago, but actually, I think he was already lost. *I* didn't lose him, because how could you lose something you never had?

I was married to a man who swore he'd never loved anyone like he loved me. He insisted my predecessors were nothing. All of the wives, even the lovers, paled in comparison to me. The poetry he spouted, gushed! You've never heard anything like it.

There were lines that still make my heart melt: 'You have ravished my heart with a glance of your eyes.' Beautiful. There were other times I thought he'd lost the plot. My teeth, a flock of sheep? They're a bit furry in the mornings, but I wouldn't go as far as to call them woolly. And when have you ever seen sheep in a straight line? 'Your nose is like a tower of Lebanon overlooking Damascus.' I didn't coo in wonder at that one. Thanks very much, I thought; if I didn't have a complex already, I will now.

He was the sexiest man on the planet. Imagine meeting the megastar you've had a crush on your whole life, terrified he'll ignore you, or worse, laugh at you. And then finding your wildest dream has come true – that he's obsessed with you. And then, even better, you get to marry him because even your father's delighted by the outcome. And you know you've won something price-less.

They were blissful weeks as the wedding inched nearer; everything was ecstasy and romance . . . then the rapturous early days of delight, both lost in a euphoric haze. We never left the bedroom. He was at his peak. Just before the midlife crisis that sent him spiralling. But by then, I was only a spectator. He dumped me like a week-old newspaper when the next one came along. I was livid. That I let myself believe I was special. That I thought it would be different with me.

Sol lived in hot pursuit of pleasure, but none he found would last. He left nothing, and no one, untried. But he couldn't sustain the rapture. All the jewels and gems and shiny things, the horses and weapons, the spices and banqueting, the wine and the women, all started to look and taste and feel the same. He was bored. And he was aging.

As he sat doling out wisdom, he started asking himself a question. One he struggled to answer. 'What's it all about?' It was like watching a tragedy and wishing it would end to put everyone out of their misery. The most captivating of men turned into a jaded old soul who wasn't satisfied with anything.

I used to have dreams that I couldn't find him. I'd hear his voice and be frantically chasing him through fields, or gardens, or streets. Like an elaborate game of hide-and-seek that only he was party to. He was lost. The wisest and richest man in this world was utterly lost.

This morning I found some of his writing, open on one of his desks: 'Enjoy life with the wife you love.' Which one of us was that, then?

The last sentence was in his own hand: 'The grand conclusion . . .' Did he know he was dying? 'The grand conclusion, when all's said and done. Give God his due and do what he says. That's what we're meant for.' I skimmed back over the pages. The great man had realized a simple truth. There's a time for everything, and we should enjoy the God-given moment, regardless of the trappings.

I could've told him that. I don't suppose he ever thought to ask. I learnt that much when I lost my place beside him. It was a gift. Short-lived.

In all his wisdom, he learned too late what he really needed to know.

Mrs Job

Job, the book called after its central character, is a hugely philosophical exploration of the subject of suffering. Here are the big theological questions, wrapped in a personal story.

Job's wife survives the horrors that are visited upon her husband, and is mentioned three times. He claims that it would be a 'heinous crime' to look at another woman and, if he were to do so, he would expect his own wife to be given to other men.[1] He, it seems, is entirely faithful to his wife. And she to him throughout their trials – however hard it must have been for her.

In the depths of his despair, Job exclaims, 'My breath is repulsive to my wife; I am loathsome to my own family.'[2] Their suffering was likely to have put huge pressure on their relationship. When all his belongings, servants and children are gone and his health soon follows, Job's wife advises, 'Do you still persist in your integrity? Curse God, and die.'[3] Having lost her ten children, I wonder if her response, born of immense pain and grief, reflects her own wish to die too.

Job replies, 'You speak as a foolish woman would speak. Shall we receive the good at the hand of God, and not receive the bad?'[4] This is the nub of the entire story, learning to accept whatever comes, without necessarily understanding why, not blaming God for it, but believing that he is all-powerful nonetheless. (Incidentally, I think she is vindicated from any *charge of female foolishness when Job's male comforters turn out to be equally, if not more, foolish). Job is the only one who emerges entirely innocent in character. Although he rails against his lot, he refuses to accuse God of wrongdoing. He believes there must be a bigger picture.*

This scene takes place after the renewal of Job's fortunes, when time has moderated the pain a little, and the benefit of hindsight has cast new light upon their sufferings. His wife is a mother again, not such a young one this time, but one with a new wisdom gained through tragedy and the acceptance of loss. Her daughters are the precocious type who like to interrupt and, as most children do, keep asking, 'Why?' I have added some of these in square brackets – not to be performed, but to show what she's dealing with. She is constantly answering their questions, which can get a little wearing.

She may be perched on the edge of a bed, and is talking to her young children. In performance, be careful not to let her sound patronizing. She believes they are old enough to hear and understand what she tells them, and deals with this story as with everything – very practically. She is reluctant to tell it at first, but decides to be completely honest with her children.

NOTES

[1] Job 31:9–12.
[2] Job 19:17.
[3] Job 2:9.
[4] Job 2:10.

Brush your teeth, Jemimah. Keren, wash your hands. And – oh, my goodness, Keziah, a clean nightie, if you please. No arguments.

Yes, we've time for a story, but only if you're quick.

(They get settled).

Right, what kind of story tonight? A true one? About who? What do you want to know about your Daddy? What a cheeky question – there's nothing wrong with his face! Oh, I see, the scars. Well, his scars are part of a much bigger story. Daddy and I had a bit of a rough ride for a while. For a long while, actually. Things got ugly. Well, yes, Daddy got ugly too when he was unwell, but that's not what I meant.

Not the whole story . . . a mummy wants to protect her little girls – you're the apple of my eye, and I want to keep you sweet and unbruised for ever. You're right, Jemimah, that is a corker of a bruise. How did you do that?

(They don't allow her to change the subject).

OK, OK. Long before you or your seven boisterous brothers were born, Daddy and I had a big house, a booming business and a lot of friends to share it with. Daddy would thank God continually for all his blessings. Then, one day, our employees and our animals were attacked and killed. It was . . . I can't really describe what we felt. As if that wasn't enough, we lost everything else in a fire. And there was far, far worse to come. We had children then, too. You had seven more brothers and three sisters who died. They were all together in Ben's house. Ben was the eldest; he had very straight teeth and was always smiling. A lovely boy. While they were eating and talking and laughing – they always had such fun together – a freak hurricane knocked the house down. They never came out.

[Why?]

We don't know why it happened, sweetie. I don't know if we ever will. God knows I've asked enough times. I was devastated – like I would be now if I lost you. You never, never forget. Daddy got down on his knees and said, 'The Lord gave and the Lord has taken away. Blessed be the name of the Lord.' I've never felt so angry, and I shouted at him, 'There are other things I could think of to say! How can you bless God when he's done this to us?'

Daddy got ill soon after. He was covered in sores from head to foot, itchy and weeping all over. A bit like the time you had the dreadful chickenpox, but a million times worse and more smelly. I told him then, 'Now's the time to give God what for and tell him he's heartless.' 'Over my dead body,' he said. 'Well,' I answered, 'looks like that moment's coming soon enough.'

He wept and he yelled until his throat was raw. He cursed the day he was born and wished he were dead. But he was certain that God was still good, even if his life wasn't. He knew his suffering wasn't fair. He still kept trying to understand why God seemed to have turned his back on us. And he begged for mercy. He was so miserable I thought he would give up breathing. I'll be honest with you, girls, he was very difficult to live with. I avoided him if I could. I was wrapped up in my own little world, grieving for my beautiful children I would never see again.

And just when I thought it couldn't get any worse, his three awful friends turned up, explaining away all our distress, and droning on as if they knew best. They said some very hurtful things.

That God was punishing Daddy and that he must have done something to deserve it.

[Why?]

I suppose they were trying to help. They didn't mean to make things worse. It's difficult to know what to say when someone is having a hard time. And at least they came and sat with him. Lots of our friends just disappeared. We never saw them for years.

[Why?]

Maybe they were scared.

[Why?]

Well, maybe they thought the bad luck might be catching.

[Why?]

Why, why, why, why, why! You're going to drive your poor mother crazy with that question!

[Why?]

Because it's the hardest question to answer.

[Why?]

Don't try my patience! There will always be more questions than answers. You will always have whys.

No, I'm afraid even Daddy doesn't know everything. His experience has given him a few more answers than before, though.

Well, when the bad times had stretched on and on, and we were drowning in despair, Daddy heard God's voice.

He said it was like a whirlwind.

What did he say? He said so many things. I'll give you the gist. 'Were you there when I made the world? Can you figure it all out? Can you make the sun rise, or tell the stars what to do? Is there any way that you could possibly know everything that I know? Do you want to argue with me?'

Well, Daddy said, 'No!' of course! He's not silly. He said it was enough for him to know that God was out there sorting out the big picture. He would learn to be patient, be quiet, and get on with praising God, whatever life threw at him.

You're right. It wasn't an *easy* answer, but I think it was a good one. It was probably a bit more poetic than that, but you know me, I don't go in for fancy-schmancy words like your dad.

Shortly after that, your father and I decided that being alive was a challenge to meet head on. We had some good long chats, said our sorries to each other, wept some more, wiped our eyes and got on with our lives. We still had each other, and that was something – the love we had always had – which had got buried under so much sorrow.

People gave us gifts to get us back on our feet; eventually, the business picked up. Your brothers came along, and then you. We are so grateful for each one of you. Nothing replaces the lives we lost, and sometimes I'm still sad. But new life brings new joy. Things are so good now, even better than they were before.

[Why?]

I think mainly because we know the alternative. You three are a beautiful, visible reminder of the turning point. 'The resurrection', as Daddy likes to call it. He never stopped saying that God would turn up. He got impatient about it, and wailed about how and when, but his faith kept him going. And his was enough to keep me going, too. So here we are. Survivors. Scarred but stronger. Answering why after why after why after why!

[Why?]

Sometimes the answer to why is just 'because'! Satisfied or not, that's all we get. I've still got plenty of questions. Some get answered in time, and I hope the rest get answered outside of time. Right now it's *time* to go to sleep.

[Why?]

Because it is. OK? I love you. Beautiful girls. I'll send Daddy up to kiss you goodnight. Sweet dreams.

Mrs Hosea

A book of Bible wives would be incomplete without a mention of Mrs Hosea – or, to use her own name, Gomer.

Hers is the most extraordinary of marriages: '. . . the LORD said to Hosea, "Go, take for yourself a wife of whoredom and have children of whoredom, for the land commits great whoredom by forsaking the LORD."'[1] In the Old Testament Scriptures, there are many occasions on which the Lord asks his prophets to act out what he wants to say to his people, but this is an extreme case!

The astounding message is that despite her continued unfaithfulness, Hosea goes on loving Gomer and even buys her back when she strays, just as God goes on loving his people and would ultimately buy them back with the death and resurrection of their Messiah. 'Go, love a woman who has a lover and is an adulteress, just as the LORD loves the people of Israel, though they turn to other gods . . . So I bought her for fifteen shekels of silver and a homer of barley and a measure of wine.'[2]

This is an exploration of the implications of Hosea's extraordinarily painful marriage. Gomer is a belligerent party animal, selling her body to all-comers to provide her with the next kick, the next thrill. Words like 'commitment', 'unselfishness' and 'generosity' don't exist in her vocabulary. How can she understand the faithful love of a man like Hosea? And what might it mean to her to be loved in that way? Perhaps it connects for the first time here, somewhere deep beneath her solid shell.

There are various ways you could choose to read or perform this. Gomer may ignore Hosea's plight and remain unchanged, continuing to hurt or pity him. In my mind, though, there is a change in her. This is her moment of transformation. Her contempt for him begins to soften when he admits how humiliated he's been. By the time she reads his letter she is moved to tears by the fact that he loves her, knowing what she is and what she's subjected him to. He is the first person to see her 'inner tears', and certainly the first to instigate their release. She leaves crying, but you can decide whether or not she decides to go back home.

NOTES

1 Hosea 1:2.
2 Hosea 3:1,2.

(Shouting back to the house she's just left).

Jez is due his milk any minute. Ru's nappy is overflowing, and will you shove a flamin' dummy in Ammi's mouth and stop his screaming? (*To herself.*) Good luck, Hosea.

(She sits/leans with a bottle of drink).

It's good to get out. I don't like being married. It's like a straitjacket. I dunno if it's marriage in general, or being married to a prophet that does it. Especially a prophet as piggin' perfect as mine. People don't get it. Yeah, all right, so I didn't *have* to marry him. But would you have turned down your one chance to escape a pimp with a fist like a hammer? Traded him in for a roof, a clean bed – and a bit of kindness? Don't judge, all right?

He turned up on my patch at festival time. Spring. New wine flowing like the River Jordan and everyone high as kites all day and night. I'd already done a ten-hour shift. Serviced plenty, made a packet. Eaten so many sacred raisin cakes for the earth goddess, I wanted to puke. Then, there he was – a bit shabby, nervous. Not like any punter I'd seen before. And I've seen them all. Paid on the spot – top price. When I asked what he was after, he said, 'I want to marry you.' I laughed in his face. Told him he needed a shrink, not a hooker.

I turned and started to walk away but he stopped me. Held my hand. His little face was pleading. Said he was acting out some kind of fantasy to show how much God loved Israel, his great whore. I said I'd heard of all kinds of kinky religious rituals, but marrying someone like me wasn't ever one of them.

Three babies later, the novelty has well and truly worn off.

You only live once, right? And it's short. I'm not settling for nappies and vomit.

He gives me cash whenever he can. Hands it over with this sad look, like I'm gonna waste it. But it's not even enough for clothes and make-up, before I start on booze and fags. Is it too much to ask for an occasional line or a pill once in a while? A girl needs a good time. It's my right to have it. So I take it.

I'm good at my job. And there are bits of it I like. I've kept working – earning a bit more than my usual 'prophet' on the side. Throwing out some freebies for the ones I like.

Hosea, the fool, always has me back when I turn up . . . He's so predictable. It makes me want to hurt him all the more.

Last night I caught him looking at me, and something snapped. I screamed at him, 'You only put up with me for the street cred – so you can keep banging on that what goes around comes around. Let's all pity poor

Hosea the martyr, making a grand old point of himself and his slutty wife, the sluttier the better.'

I waited. Then he blew, like a volcano.

'You don't get it, do you?' He was whacking his fist on the table. 'You just don't get it.' He said it might've been pity or a promise or whatever it was at first. But that now he can't face living without me, whatever I get up to. He was yelling, 'I know I should throw you out, but I can't. I just can't. I love you.'

Pathetic! I wasn't going to let him make me feel bad about myself. I only do what comes natural. 'What if you get something from me? What if I make you ill? Doesn't that frighten you?'

He looked spent. Slumped at the table. Said every time he "makes love" to me, he hears his mother's voice saying, 'Leave it alone, you don't know where it's been.' And that it drives him crazy when I leave every night. That there's not a bloke in Israel that doesn't know my body at least as well as he does. He had his head in his hands – I reckon he was trying to hide his tears. 'Don't you understand how much it humiliates me? I've given you everything I have to give – even my self-respect. There's nothing left.'

He hasn't spoken since. I did nothing but give him the bare minimum of instructions before I slammed the door. As I was leaving, he shoved this note in my bag.

(She takes out a crumpled piece of paper).

'My precious Gomer, I'm so sorry if I said anything to wound or hurt you last night. It's the last thing I meant to do. I don't know where you'll go tonight, who you'll be with, or why, but I'd give anything to heal your pain and wipe away those inner tears that no one else sees. So come home to me, my darling, before my heart is completely broken. And there will be no questions, no anger, no reproach – only my arms open wide and waiting for you.'

Mrs Jonah

The book of Jonah is compact and beautifully written. The story, with its absurd turn of events, could be one of the best known in the Bible. Jonah runs away from the challenge God sets out for him, so the Almighty takes drastic measures to sort him out. He whips up a storm, and has Jonah thrown overboard and swallowed by a big fish, where he has three days to think about his actions before being vomited onto dry ground and sent back to try to achieve his mission.

Jonah's prayer of thanksgiving in chapter 2 is moving and exultant. Here is a man who knows, loves and hears God, and is not in the habit of running away. Excuse the awful pun, but I think the fishy part of the story is a red herring. Jonah's resistance to doing what he is told is actually due to his horror of Nineveh, a large city renowned for its injustice, brutality and aggression. But God still cares for the locals there, and sends Jonah to warn them of the disaster that will arrive in forty days, unless they change their ways. The warning is heeded and the inhabitants are transformed. 'When God saw what they did, how they turned from their evil ways, God changed his mind about the calamity that he had said he would bring upon them; and he did not do it.'[1]

In response, Jonah becomes really angry, 'O LORD! Is not this what I said while I was still in my own country? That is why I fled to Tarshish at the beginning; for I knew that you are a gracious God and merciful, slow to anger, and abounding in steadfast love, and ready to relent from punishing.'² Jonah avoided his calling because he would rather see the inhabitants of Nineveh destroyed. That is the shocking heart of the story, which is all too human and easy to relate to today.

God gently reveals the quality of his love to Jonah when the bush that gives him shelter from the sun dies in the heat of the day. *'You are concerned about the bush, for which you did not labour and which you did not grow . . . And should I not be concerned about Nineveh, that great city, in which there are more than a hundred and twenty thousand people who do not know their right hand from their left, and also many animals?'³* Jonah knows God is merciful, but he can't quite get his head around it, because the forgiving nature of that love is so different from his own instincts.

Here, Mrs Jonah is the type of woman who likes to do the questionnaires and quizzes in women's mags. She is excited by the idea of adventures, but doesn't believe they happen in her own life. She cares deeply for her husband, but struggles to communicate, as many women do, with a man who is a natural loner and so easily withdraws into himself. She earnestly prays for him and, because he listens to God more than to her, her prayers probably work.

NOTES

[1] Jonah 3:10.
[2] Jonah 4:2.
[3] Jonah 4:10,11.

(Flicking through a magazine).

"Is your man telling the truth?" Bingo.

(Reading). 'A cheating man is often given away by his face. Either blushing or seeming excessively pale can be a sign of the strain of lying. Darting eyes or, indeed, a concerted effort not to blink excessively, might be the giveaway. Touching the mouth, tugging the ears or agitated hand movements can all indicate a dishonest response. He might parrot your questions, change the subject, or think for too long about the answers to your queries.' Good grief! That could be every conversation we've ever had.

(She throws down the magazine).

This is no good. It doesn't have a paragraph on the actual chances of your husband setting off on a spontaneous boat trip, then being thrown overboard and swallowed by a giant fish before being vomited on the beach back home three days later.

I told him, 'I just want you to be honest!' He was silent. I pleaded with him, 'What are you thinking?' and he huffed, 'Nothing!' Like he always does. He must be thinking *something*. Why do men always insist that there is absolutely nothing going on in their heads? Maybe there isn't. But in my head the answer is, 'I'm thinking of things far too complex for you to understand,' or 'I'm thinking of things I wouldn't dream of sharing with you,' or 'I'm thinking your bum looks big in that.'

I told him, 'I think we need to talk. About us.' He groaned. 'This isn't the moment, woman! I've had a nightmare of a trip and I've another one to go on.' So I asked, 'Where now? Africa? Want to be swallowed by a lion this time? Only I've heard they have bigger teeth than fish!' 'Nineveh,' he sighs.

I've always wanted to go. That great city. Three days just to walk across it. Thousands of people, the lights, the smells, the clubs, the buzz. Although people don't usually come back; it lures you in, or traps you. And it's dangerous. There are people there who think nothing of pulling out all your fingernails one by one.

I nagged him into opening up. Harried him till he didn't have the energy to resist. It was quicker than usual. Apparently, three days in the belly of a big fish will take the fight right out of a person. I told him, 'You don't even *like* fish, you won't touch it when I cook it.' 'Tell me about it!' he shouts back. 'I don't think it was a revenge attack!'

We sat down and he talked and I can't tell you the relief. Just to hear what's going on behind those worried eyes and feel like he'd let me in a little bit. Turns out, God's been speaking to him. 'Is that all?' I was relieved. '*All*, woman? Is that *all*?' He shouts. 'If God wants me to go to that hole and tell them he's seen their wickedness, likelihood is he wants to forgive them and, frankly, I don't think they deserve that chance.' The root of the matter. Jonah knows better than God. I had to stifle a giggle; he ends up swallowed by a fish when he didn't even need to get in a boat! Nineveh is across land, out east in Assyria, but in his disgust at the thought of it, Jonah goes to the docks and heads west to Spain. The doofus.

He's had a thing against Ninevites since for ever. Says they're without exception debauched and depraved. I did say, 'Jonah, sweetheart, for a first, that's a mighty big brush you're painting with. Let it go – it must be heavy. For a second, you've never been there. You've never met a Ninevite. Don't you think you're being a teensy bit . . . well, a bit of a bigot, frankly?' 'This is why I don't talk to you!' he yells. 'You don't understand!'

I do, actually. I understand. I get it. Their godlessness winds him up tight enough to snap *and* he's not street-wise. He's scared they'll eat him for dinner. Once they've pulled his nails out.

But he's gone this morning and I'm glad. If I know Jonah, he'll sulk all the way, but at least he's gone to tell them that God's on their case. The God of second chances. The God who gave Jonah a second chance to do what he was told, so you'd think he'd be sympathetic.
Please God, keep him safe. And please keep speaking to him, show him that you made those people and you

love them. And please God, can you save Ninevah so that I can go there one day? Just for the shopping; I don't fancy a manicure. And God, when he gets home, will you help him to talk to me properly, and tell me the truth? Swallowed by a big fish. I mean, really. Really?

NEW
TESTAMENT

Miss Shepherd

The Christmas story in Matthew and Luke's gospels is so famil-iar, it can be hard to find new ways of approaching a much-rehearsed and well-loved account.

This is a new take on the story – a fictional female shepherd elaborating on the description given by the (presumably male) shepherds whom we know visited the infant Jesus soon after his birth.[1]

Being a shepherd was not a desirable job. It was hard work, badly paid, and a lonely existence. This young shepherdess is already jaded by the drudgery and isola-tion in which she feels trapped. But when an opportunity for a very different kind of a life arises, will she be able to take a risk and leave behind the only security she knows?

She is outdoors and probably well wrapped up. She might have a flower or branch in her hand that she is absent-mind-edly pulling apart as she talks. In my mind, she's Welsh. The tuneful lilt of a rural accent allows for a lot of expression in the voice, as does the fact that she is still young and uninhibited. She thinks in the moment of speaking, rather than ahead of time. Her speech is addressed to an attentive listener, a close friend, whose identity remains a mystery until the end.This piece could be performed by a man if you imagine Seth as a friend rather than her partner, and remove the references to weddings.

NOTE

1   Luke 2:8–20.

I hate being a shepherd. It stinks. In more ways than one. Stuck out here. Freezing my backside off. Bored out of my brain. Sorry, am I dragging you down? That's not fair. It's not your fault I'm here.

I can't help it. I've been feeling absolutely rotten since three days ago. You probably guessed. I've been dying for something – *anything* – to look forward to. Me and Seth have been together a few years now, as you know. I keep thinking we should have a wedding, give us something to talk about. But we can't afford one, so pointless talk is all it is. Pointless talk.

It's this thing that happened a few days ago. It's unsettled me. You weren't here. I think you were down in the valley at the time, getting water. It was up on the peak, quite late. Seth and I, we were chatting with some of the shepherds from the other side of the mountain, swapping a bit of gossip and whatever. When this blinding ball of flame shot out of the sky right at us!

Turned out to be some kind of person that looked as if they were made out of light. I know! I thought I'd died. Then, it spoke! Said, 'Don't be afraid!' I thought, well, that's easy for you to say! You've probably got used to being you, but I can't help finding you a *little* bit scary! It was broadcasting something about a baby just born down in Bethlehem who's the Saviour. My first thought was that my mother meant it all those times she sang to me, 'You'd better not shout, you'd better not frown, because the Messiah's coming to town.'

The whatever-it-was said it had good news, fantastic news for everyone. And I thought, pull the other one, shiny-man, shepherds never get good news! Then this awesome choir piped up from behind him, better than *X Factor*. They were singing, 'Glory to God, and peace on earth to all those he approves.' I got the feeling they meant *we* were approved. That can't be right because no one approves of a shepherd, do they? Shepherds are the ones with no prospects. The ones with no excitement. The ones that go do-lally from being so far out of the action. The ones that don't even get a proper wedding.

Seth and the others jumped up to go, and we argued. I said *someone* had to keep an eye out up here. *Someone* had to be sensible or we'd all get fired, and where would that leave us?

He couldn't understand why I wouldn't want to go on an adventure. Why I wouldn't want to see a turning point in history. Why, when given an opportunity, I wouldn't want to be in on something life-changing.

(Realizing.) Thinking about it . . . I don't know, either.

I'm not the quickest of thinkers. They all just upped and left. It was once they'd gone I thought maybe I should've . . . What do you think?

They've been telling everyone about it. In all the pubs – any excuse. They reckon the messenger was an angel, and turns out what he said was absolutely right. They found the baby exactly like he said and they've been praising God right, left and centre ever since, saying this baby is going to change the world.

And I missed it.

It's nice to have someone to talk to about it all. What would you do?

(Pause. She realizes there's still time).

You're right. He's not going to disappear, is he? That's not what babies do. He's going to grow up, isn't he? That's what babies do.

(She makes the decision to go).

OK, you lot, Baa-bara's in charge. Because she's the oldest, don't argue! Lambert, are you coming with me? Brilliant, let's go! Better late than never.

(Sigh). Sometimes I think you sheep are the only ones who understand me.

Mrs Balthasar

It is recorded that after the birth of Jesus, Joseph and Mary received various visitors, including some who brought unusual gifts. Matthew tells us that three gifts were given by 'wise men from the East'.[1] Since the eighth century, three names have been assigned to the Magi[2] in Western Christianity: Balthasar, Caspar or Gaspar, and Melchior. Imagining that at least one of them was married, we've sent Mrs Balthasar on the journey with them – which was certainly possible. She was no doubt a comfortable, middle-class lady, whose horizons would have been very constrained by the culture in which she lived. Being swept away on an unexpected adventure came as a complete surprise. Remembering the journey years later, she is able to find an exciting sense of purpose beyond her domesticity.

She assumes the caller at the door will leave quickly and is reluctant to talk at first, but as he coaxes the story from her and she begins to share it, she realizes how desperate she has been to tell it. We don't know if she has children, but she is certainly motherly.

NOTES

[1]   Matthew 2:1–12.

2   'Magi', of Persian origin, was used to describe this religious
    group with an international reputation for astrology.

(She opens the door to a stranger, and answers his questions).

Yes? You're a what? And who do you write for? I'm afraid my husband's out. I doubt I can help.

What do you want to know?

Oh no, I've never liked travelling. I much prefer to stay on the sofa, safe from the elements. Besides, there's no need. Babylon has everything a woman could want – I've got temples, theatres, restaurants and shopping right on my doorstep. Balthasar travels, but he has something to offer. What's the point in *me* going anywhere? I have nothing to say that anyone needs to hear. I'm sure I'll be of no use to you.

No, really.

(Reluctantly). Oh, all right. Come in, and I'll answer your questions if I can.

Yes, my husband is quite famous – astrology – he has a lot of brain cells but little conversation. While I'm watching the soaps, he studies the stars and planets and anything they point to. Which seems to include deities and so forth. I don't take a keen interest.

No, never. Well . . . there was once.

It was a long time ago. I shouldn't . . . I haven't . . . It was the only time I did go on a journey, a long one, by camel. I remember it as if it were yesterday. Probably because my backside never recovered.

Why do you want to know?

(She thinks and eventually decides to tell the story).

OK. The whole thing? From the beginning? Well. *(Thinking to herself.)* Where did it start?

(She launches in).

For some time, my other half had been studying the religion of the Hebrews, who live some way out west. I took him a bite to eat and he was muttering, 'A remarkable people. With a remarkable history. And still waiting. For some kind of leader or messiah to secure their freedom.' Well, poor them, I thought for a second, then promptly forgot about them when I went to wash up.

Then a friend of Balthasar's came to stay. The two of them spent days and nights discussing some major new thrilling phenomenon in the sky. Yawn. For a man of few words, my husband had an awful lot to say on this particular subject. From what I understood, a series of signs seemed to be forming some kind of pattern that meant something big was about to happen. World impacting. As long as it doesn't impact me it can do what it likes, I thought.

'Very soon,' Balthasar confided, 'we'll have another visitor.' 'Pull the other one,' I laughed, and then there was a loud knocking at the door. 'If Gaspar agrees with us, we must take action,' my husband said. Gaspar was a huge man with a big bushy black beard. 'Don't bother unpacking my bag,' he commanded, marching past me without as much as a by your leave. 'Pack theirs, woman. We have to stop looking at the stars and start following one!'

Pack the bags! Woman! What am I, a skivvy? You see, that's the trouble with wise men; they're not always wise when it comes to the basics. If I didn't go with them to see to the food, they'd starve before they were halfway there.

They were as excited as schoolboys. A new star in the sky, and a big one at that! Well, whoopee. 'We have to go and find the great king born under this star and take him gifts,' Balthasar explained. He's very patient with me. 'You know, just like the Queen of Sheba took gifts to King Solomon of Israel.' 'Right. So I'm the Queen of Sheba, then?' No answer.

I started to regret my decision as soon as it was made. That kind of thing just isn't me. But I chose to grin and bear it. If it was good enough for the Queen of Sheba . . . I've never forgotten a detail. We travelled east to west in a long caravan – not one of those ones that's a mini house on wheels with miraculous tables that fold into beds. Sadly . . . it was just a ragtag procession on camels. Stubborn ones.

And we took gifts with us: gold, frankincense and myrrh, in caskets covered in jewels. 'Myrrh?' I said. 'Isn't that the stuff they use to embalm bodies? What's wrong with Chanel Number 5?' Wise men, I ask you! But no one listens to the cook and bottle washer. One good thing: the waft of myrrh would ward off any self-respecting bandits en route. And it went some way to masking the reek of Gaspar's socks.

By day I was pining for home and wondering what I was doing. By night I was amazed at the stars. I came close to understanding Balthasar's passion.

We arrived in Jerusalem. J-e-r-u- . . . Jerusalem, yes. It's the capital, so the boys thought we'd made it. We got to the palace and it was very nice, even if not to my taste. Bit chintzy. Everyone was all smiles and watching their p's and q's. Except for Gaspar, who couldn't help but bark, 'So where's the new king?' Silence. I sensed the atmosphere was a bit tense. 'A new king? Herod is our king – alive and kicking. (And with secret police everywhere.)' 'We're not afraid of him,' Balthasar said. 'We are scholars. We teach kings and governments their job!' I noticed that didn't stop his knees knocking as we went into the throne room.

But King Herod seemed at ease. He sent for his advisors who said prophecy in the Jewish Scriptures pointed to Bethlehem as the birthplace of this new king. So we were six miles out. I think that moment was the closest any of them have been to asking for directions.

I'd have loved to have stayed for a bath, but the boys wanted to push on. Herod was most insistent that when we found the little chap we let him know, so that he could go and pay his respects, too. 'Of course we will, we will indeed,' they said. Why are wise men so easily taken in? Herod was so oily that we sailed out of the room on a slick.

Should I carry on? Is this the sort of story you'd like to know?

The star that had led us all the way from Babylon took us to a place where a local innkeeper kept his cattle. Snuggled in the straw was a very . . . unremarkable young couple, with a baby. I thought, if this is a king, then I *am* the Queen of Sheba. She let me hold him. The sense of peace. I forgot everything else, including home. My backside even stopped hurting.

My husband and his two friends fell to their knees right there in the dung, and began weeping and thanking God. The parents seemed a tad surprised. Well, three big, hairy, blubbing men are on the unexpected side, I suppose.

They accepted the gifts and thanked us profusely. Gold is fit for a king and useful, obviously. Frankincense they'll use for sacrifice in worship, I suppose. But I don't think they knew any more than I did what the myrrh was for. You don't give funeral gifts at a christening, do you? How embarrassing.

The boys were so excited I couldn't get them to bed. I'd only just dozed off when Balthasar shook us all awake again saying, 'Get up. We've got to set off quick and cover our tracks. I think we're in real danger.' He said he knew from a dream. Remembering Herod's eyes, I believed he was right. My first thought was for the baby. Balthasar took me in his arms. 'God has gone to such trouble to bring us here, we have to trust him to look after the baby.' My second thought was, Oh grief, I've got to get back on that camel.

Camels can run faster than you think. I was holding on for dear life, wondering if this danger was worse than the other. We got home in half the time, but with double the bruises.

I'm no more keen on travelling than I was. But I can't deny it was worth it. I may have damaged my rear end, but at least I wasn't just sitting on it.

I've wondered what happened to that baby almost every day. But we've kept completely silent for fear of the child's safety. This is the first time I've told anyone.

We heard a few years later that Herod was dead. Since then, another forty have passed. That baby might be a king by now, and kings have annals, don't they? A record of what goes on. So I should speak up, shouldn't I? To make sure they get all the details.

Oh, you are? Will it be published? What did you say your name was?

Will you be including my part of the story, do you think, Matthew?

Golly. Balthasar will wonder that for once his wife stood up to be counted.

Yes, put in anything you like. And will you send me a copy? I'd like to know what happened next, and whether the myrrh was a total mistake.

Really?

Let me get the kettle on, Matthew. You can tell me all about it.

Mrs Newlywed

Jesus turning water into wine is arguably one of the best known and favourite miracles. In John's gospel it isn't called a miracle, it's called a 'sign'. John records seven of these signs that Jesus performed, all indicating that he was the Messiah. This is the first. We're told it 'revealed his glory; and his disciples believed in him.'[1]

This was not a public display or show. Not everyone witnessed it. Most of the guests were unaware of the source of the bountiful and delicious new wine. Interestingly, although it would be an embarrassment for the host not to provide enough wine at a wedding, it was still more of a luxury than a necessity. And Jesus doesn't do generosity by half. We're told there were six jars of up to thirty gallons of wine, which makes a maximum of 819 litres. In today's terms, that adds up to 1,092 bottles. Even with a lower alcoholic percentage than we are used to, that would seem fairly extravagant, even reckless. A wedding party lasted several days, up to a week, with continual drinking throughout.

In the passage,[2] we read who was party to the incident: Jesus' mother requests his input, his friends are witnesses, the servants fetch the water and serve it up, the head steward tastes it, and then he consults the bridegroom about its quality. The bride may have been blissfully unaware of the social faux pas that

Jesus so graciously and generously averted. She would have been very young, little more than a girl, with all the usual one-upmanship of any new bride. She is the type who likes to have her finger on the pulse of what is going on, and to offer her opinion, even when it's not requested.

Here she is talking to the young Joanna, and then also to her new husband, turning from one to the other. I think she is a bit miffed at the end to have been trumped on her wedding planning skills.

NOTES

[1] John 2:11.
[2] John 2:1–11.

(Entering the room).

There are so many ways to make a wedding go with a bang, Joanna, and there's no need to break the bank. We had a great time on a seriously limited budget. I'm glad your mum sent you to me. And just in time – this morning the photos arrived! Come and sit, let's see.

(They look through the wedding album).

Oh, look, Dad looks so nervous. That's my dress. Worn before by a few other people, but you'd never know. Mum and I made some alterations. This is the first day, so everyone is still looking pristine.

There he is. Look at that. You have to admit, he's a fine specimen. Would you look at the shape of him – the ripple of his arms, the swell of his chest! Stop me if this is inappropriate, but oh, the line of his jaw, that winning smile . . . I'm not being lecherous, I'm just saying . . . God excelled himself with that one.

No, no, that's the best man, the *other* one is James. The one with his hair sticking up and the squiffy eye, *that's* my new husband. His gorgeous mate's already taken.

I'll be honest, I wasn't sure about James at first. He's clearly no work of art. But he is a good man, so I stuck with him. And we have a lot of fun together. Then, during the wedding, I realized that I actually am in love with him. And I noticed it despite the fact that he was pretty hammered for most of the week – so that's a good sign, I think.

His job was to provide the wine, and he excelled himself. I was so proud! Look at them all, toasting and cheering and dancing.

Was that the door? Yay! James is home!

Jamie, come and see the wedding photos, they got here this morning. This is Joanna. Her mum was at our do and has sent her to talk weddings and find out the secrets of laying on a really good one. I've been telling her a fab party like ours needn't cost the earth. You just need good wine, and lots of it, right?

What? Don't be ridiculous, we didn't run out. He's just teasing. Jamie, you're such a kidder! He got it on sale or return to keep costs to a minimum. We can't possibly have got through the lot . . .

Yes, I remember your dad's cousin – Auntie Mary, right? The one with the posse of burly boys. *(To Joanna)*. She was overseeing the serving for us. One of her sons is just launching a career as a rabbi. She reckons he's really going places, very avant-garde. *(To James)*. He told the servants to do what?

That's disgusting. There's no way they would've served up the washing water. It's foul and has bits floating in it. I think I would've noticed if someone had tried to give me that, right, Joanna? No one would drink it.

(She hears these lines from James and repeats them to Joanna).

It miraculously turned into wine.
And I didn't notice at the time.
And it was the best wine I've ever tasted.
And there was plenty of it.
Stop repeating . . . I'm not repeating everything you say. Well, maybe I am, but I'm feeling a bit incredulous, Jamie! Did he do the cappuccinos, too? What did he make them out of? Don't tell me, he got all the waiters to spit into the toilet bowl and hey presto. Come off it. Tell me the truth now, no jokes.

Oh, no. I bet the supplier was fuming that you'd out-sourced a thousand bottles. Has he said anything yet? With any luck, he was too drunk to notice.

Does everybody know that's what happened? Good job! I'd be mortified! Then why did he do it? We should hope he doesn't call it in, we couldn't return a favour like that!

(She considers the situation).

Well, Joanna, sorry not to be more help, but I'm afraid I have nothing more to say. Isn't that right, Jamie? Turns out that I have no advice to give except that if you want a swinging wedding, you should make sure to invite Jesus of Nazareth!

Mrs Zacchaeus

Zacchaeus was a collector of taxes – one of the richest and most hated men in the area, as he no doubt made his wealth by oppression, bribery and corruption. A little man in both size and stature, he couldn't appear in public without drawing the jeers of the crowds; so he decides to take a surreptitious peek at the famous new rabbi by hiding himself in a tree.

But Jesus, the fun-loving Messiah, knows he's there and shouts his good news to this creep of a little man for all to hear: 'Come down from the tree, Zacchaeus, me and the lads are going to party at your house today!'[1]

What a shock for the onlookers – that Jesus would eat with such a wretch of a man! What an embarrassment for Zacchaeus, to climb down in front of them. But nowhere are we told whether Mrs Zacchaeus was pleased.

What did this woman think? She has lived with the man for some time, knows all the unpleasant details of his miserable life and, in a moment, he is completely transformed. 'Today salvation has come to this house,'[2] declares Jesus, and then makes an astounding claim that he 'came to seek out and to save the lost.'[3] The Word on the Street translation is, 'I'm here to track down the missing persons and re-introduce them to life.'[4]

When the party is over, Zacchaeus pulls an impressive U-turn, refocuses and puts right his wrongs. I've called it a 'personality transplant', and I've seen it happen in apparently impossible situations. Meeting Jesus can transform even those who appear past help.

I've thought of Zacchaeus's wife as a tired and slightly hung over, middle-class mother who's been denied the life she dreams of because she's married to a miserable skinflint. She is taken aback and really put out that her husband has changed now, with no help from her, when she's been trying to instigate a change for so long. She is eventually delighted . . . but only once she has come to terms with the idea that the change is positive, regardless of how it came about.

When performing this live, don't introduce it with the title or any description of who she is, because it will spoil the humour of the revelation midway.

NOTES

[1] See Luke 19:5.
[2] Luke 19:9.
[3] Luke 19:10.
[4] Rob Lacey, *The Word on the Street* (Grand Rapids, MI: Zondervan, 2003), p. 304.

(She's in a park, shouting to her children whilst retreating to a bench or other observation point. She meets a neighbour, and strikes up a conversation).

Hetty, not head first, sit on your bottom! No, roundabouts make me sick, Jake. Mummy needs to take five, OK? (Two aspirin and three Prozac).

Hello. Are you new to the area? Nice to meet you. Which one's yours? Sweet.

(To Jake). You sat in what? No, you can't just wipe it on your sister!

(To the neighbour). There's another pair of dungarees that'll need a miracle. Crown me the queen of make-do and mend. I hope you're settling in. Who've you met so far? Sour old Sol? Don't let the kids kick a ball into his garden, you'll never get it back. Rowdy Rebecca? You hear her before you see her, but it's nice to have the warning. And no doubt you've met the tax man, Zacchaeus. I'll bet he was standing at the door checking off your furniture on the way in, salivating over the sums. Comes to collect the tax on Tuesdays and Wednesdays. And Fridays. And Sundays. Never takes a day off. Money makes him weak at his tiny little knees. You must've met him. Little beady eyes. But you don't want to look him in the eye for too long, it gives you a bad back. That man won't buy a new toilet roll until the old one's finished and the cardboard's been used. He is a vile little wretch of a man. A mean-as-mean no-good.

Oh yes, I've known him for ages. He's my husband. Years and years I've been trying to change that man. I've tried everything. Completely unchangeable. His obsession grips our family like a vice. We never have people round. It would be like charity, he says, and 'We are not a charity.'

Then, get this – this is why I'm feeling . . . a little *delicate*, shall we say. Last night, out of nowhere, he waltzes in with a heaving crowd of assorted freaks and weirdos, and announces, 'My darling! Dinner for everyone!' I nearly fainted in shock. He's never called me 'darling'. I had nothing in the oven, nothing in the fridge, nothing in the freezer, and all these madly grinning northern oiks were making me nervous. Not to mention the effect on my carpet.

Zac whispers, 'Keep them talking – I'll nip to Waitrose and buy something special.' Waitrose he'll nip to! Waitrose! He only ever lets me shop in Lidl! He brought back flowers. This is the man who calls flowers 'an unnecessarily overpriced, needlessly wasteful gesture you can well live without'. And he danced around the house – *danced*, I jest not – all evening, recklessly topping up glasses with Chateauneuf-du-Cana – which wasn't on special offer!

So we're having this wild, impromptu party, and Zac's an entirely different person. He's throwing money at people. He's like someone I'd actually like to be married to!

I blame that Jesus. One meeting with him, and he's instantly a new man.

Years! Years of hard graft I've put in, trying to make Zac at least a little pleasant occasionally. It's put me in mind of a stiff lid on a jar. I must've been loosening it all these years, so Jesus could just come along and . . . 'pop'. Infuriating.

I don't know why I'm complaining. I think I . . . well it's just, I mean . . .

Yes, it was a wonderful party. I guess I just . . . I don't know, I . . .

You're right. I have a new husband. Apparently Jesus makes a habit of this kind of thing. He calls it 'seeking and saving the lost'. I call it a personality transplant. I mean, look at him on that roundabout! That's not normal, is it? He's actually having fun. I've never seen the kids laughing so hard.

Will you excuse me? I think I'm going to join in.

Mrs Ten

Although now rare and easily manageable, in biblical times leprosy was such a contagious skin disease that sufferers were confined to isolation camps and ostracized from public life. Leprosy causes the skin's surface to become uneven and to whiten. Eventually, the nerves fail so injuries become hard to avoid. In biblical culture, leprosy was also seen as a sign of God's displeasure, a spiritual disease caused by sin. Jesus had no problem socializing with all of society's least desirables, even if the religious leaders and the well-to-do resented him for it. He is also recorded as frequently healing people – whenever he was requested to do so.

Luke tells us that on his way to Jerusalem, Jesus was passing through a village between Samaria and Galilee, and is approached by ten lepers who beg him for mercy. They are all healed, but only one returns to thank him.[1] This is his story – and that of his wife, of course. In this piece she is an articulate and fervent campaigner, a little over-serious, and probably nervous about giving a public speech. She is completely unaware of the comedy in some of her language choices.

It is a tongue-in-cheek piece. If performing live you may need to be aware of the sensibilities of those present. It won't suit every palate, and this type of humour may not be appropriate in some situations. In informal settings, it could work really well.

NOTE

¹ Luke 17:11–19.

Good evening. Firstly, I'd like to thank you for inviting me to speak. As you will hear, Protection from Every Effect of Leprosy is a charity close to my heart. I've been familiar with the work of PEEL ever since my husband was diagnosed with a skin disorder eight years ago, just five months after our wedding. Within a few days, his condition was confirmed and he was confined to an isolation camp on the north border of Samaria. We've been separated ever since.

It took me some time to get used to being alone in our home. I missed him dreadfully, and wasn't much comforted by the small pieces of him I had kept in a jar. Visits to the camp were like hell on earth. Even if you have no experience of living with leprosy, I'm sure you can imagine the emotional torment that exceeds even the physical distress. I've been campaigning for many years for a better understanding of the realities of life with leprosy, and for improved conditions for sufferers. But this evening I'm here to tell you there's a new light at the end of the tunnel, a definitive scratch for that itch.

Over the years, my husband David has tried every possible remedy; from mud treatments to chemicals, from freezing to fire, from surgery to herbal supplements. The fact is, leprosy was here to stay, but his skin wasn't. Until last week! Last week, he reached a decision that action was vital, even if it put himself and others at risk.

He had heard of a rabbi called Jesus who has been healing the sick around the country, all sorts of ailments, including the worst ailment of all, death. He figured leprosy might be an easy one for someone like that.

So, he rallied nine of his co-sufferers and convinced them to escape the camp for a last-ditch attempt at freedom. Unfortunately, several of them left behind bits of . . . themselves on the barbed wire, so they were noticed and pursued. When they got to the village where Jesus was, they were exhausted but elated and, remembering to keep a safe distance lest they infect their last hope, David shouted, and the others joined in: 'Jesus, please have mercy on us.'

He walked right up to them. No fear. He touched each of them. Several cried at the first human contact they'd had since they could remember. He told them to go and show themselves to the priest, which didn't go down all that well. Most of them have a phobia of priests since the last time they saw one they were condemned to the life sentence of leper. But what do you do when you've tried everything else?

Off they went, as fast as they could, for fear of the officials in pursuit. When they got to the priest's house, they summoned the courage to knock on the door. David was looking down at his feet, as he always does, and noticed his missing toes were back where they should be, and there wasn't the usual dusty debris of his own skin around him. He looked at his hand and its colour was normal. He felt his face and it was smooth. He hammered on the door so hard his knuckles stung, and when it was opened begged to look in a mirror. It's not usually the first thing people ask to do at the priest's house. After a kerfuffle and some explanations, there was a thorough examination. (My eyes water just thinking about it). It was followed by lots of hearty back-slapping (now that they could all do that without fear of unpleasant consequences). The priest declared them all clean and fit.

As they were leaving, the officials turned up to cart them back to the camp, but couldn't take a single one now they all had a clean bill of health. It was a triumphant moment.

They all ran off in different directions to do the things they'd been dreaming of, and see the loved ones they'd been longing for. David didn't come straight home to me.

I'm not upset, though, because he's well brought up. He ran right back in the direction he'd come and found Jesus to say thank you. I'm glad he did. I would've insisted on sending a card at least, it's only polite. David had done so much running by this time I think he tripped and ended up lying on the floor at Jesus' feet, weeping and thanking him. Jesus didn't seem to mind in the slightest that a former leper, and a Samaritan to boot, was slobbering all over his sandals. He asked where the other nine were and David didn't know. He just said again and again how grateful he was that God had given him another chance, and he would never forget it. Jesus said, 'You can go on your way, your faith has made you well.' And well he is. He is completely whole again, every missing bit returned, every broken bit fixed, and his will to live restored.

I can't adequately describe how it feels to have him back, to be reunited now that his illness no longer keeps us apart. I thought I would never feel his touch again, and now we can share a bed once more.

We've been back to visit the camp David escaped from, that had become his identity. There are still people there who need hope. I implore you to pray for those still suffering. Our campaigning with PEEL carries on apace, in the knowledge that Prevention of Every Effect of Leprosy is now an achievable goal. The cure is Jesus of Nazareth. We thank God for him.

In fact, I believe gratitude has changed our lives even more than healing; we now enjoy every moment, knowing that whether hard done by or blessed in this life, we don't get what we deserve. So, for each trial and mercy, thanks is due. And I thank you for listening to me and, in hope, I thank you for supporting PEEL. It may be that you decide to ignore me entirely, or disbelieve my story. To that I say, it's no skin off my nose, it's yours you need to worry about.

Mrs Nicodemus

It is in a night-time conversation between a learned man called Nicodemus and Jesus that arguably the most famous Bible verse is embedded. Jesus tells him, 'For God so loved the world that he gave his only Son, so that everyone who believes in him may not perish but may have eternal life.'[1]

Their discussion is also the source of the much used and debated phrase, 'born again'. Nicodemus's question, 'Can one enter a second time into the mother's womb and be born?'[2] might make any woman say 'Ouch'! Did this line of thought worry his wife and mother?

Nicodemus was an important man as a member of the ruling council of the Pharisees and the strong opposition of his colleagues to Jesus could be the reason he went to talk with him in the dead of night. A little later he speaks up for Jesus, though with little real force or effect, suggesting he should be questioned before being condemned.[3] He is later found with Joseph of Arimathea burying Jesus after the crucifixion.[4]

Nicodemus and Joseph of Arimathea are the only two Pharisees who seem to make any positive response to Jesus, but they appear unable to follow their convictions and defend him with any success. It may well have been agonizing to face this battle between their instincts and their position. It may even have posed a threat to their families.

In this piece, Mrs Nicodemus is Irish. She has the gift of the blarney, and is on the telephone. What the Irish accent adds could also be achieved with enthusiasm and rhythm of delivery. She says exactly what she's thinking and talks quickly because her mind is ahead of her mouth.

NOTES

1   John 3:16.
2   John 3:4.
3   John 7:50,51.
4   John 19:38–40.

(On the telephone).

Mammy, it's me. How are you? Is it a good time? Ach, don't ask. I'm worried about that husband of mine.

I remember, you told me on the morning of me wedding, it's a wife's lot to worry! You know how proud I am of him since he's been on the council of Pharisees. He's worked so hard to get there, and he's so well respected. I thought there'd be nothing but promotion to come, you know? But recently he's been a bit shifty and murmuring about swimming against the tide and so on. Then about a week ago, I woke up in the night, and he was gone! He'd crept off somewhere in the dark. He wouldn't tell me where for ages. Said he was protecting me. I started to worry he was up to no good. So I pulled a bit of a strop and eventually he comes clean, making me promise I'd keep it a secret.

Well, he's not the bravest of men, is he?

You'll never guess . . . He'd been away to see this Jesus that everyone's talking about.

I know! Said he had to speak with him for himself. Well, let me tell you, since then he's been even stranger.

Things he's saying mostly. He's been asking me questions about childbirth, and if I think you can be born twice.

That's what I said. One labour's bad enough. But he said he was talking about a spiritual birth as well as a physical one. And how God wants us to be born spiritually. Well, I don't know what he means but he makes me feel like I was born yesterday. I can't follow it for the life of me.

Then, it gets worse Ma, he starts talking about eternal life and such. And I'm guessing he means life after death because it's quite clear our bodies are on a downhill slide already.

He stopped me dead in the kitchen yesterday and looked me straight in the eyes, all wild and desperate, like. And he begged me to trust him when he said that Jesus had come to save us from eternal death if we only believed in him. I was a bit scared. He said he was just super-keen that I understand what he'd just understood. I'm used to him zealous, but this feels a bit different.

I suppose I feel like he's left me behind a bit. I'm scared that soon I won't know him at all. And there's the council to worry about. They're not signed-up members of the Jesus fan club like my hubby. I'm praying he'll do nothing stupid. He's talking about upholding justice and making sure there's a fair hearing.

I know it doesn't *sound* bad, but it's not the way these things go when the council have made their mind up. I never thought religious leadership would be such a risky business. I had a strange man round here a wee while ago claiming he was checking our drainage was regulation. No one's ever given a second look to our drainage. But he says *no one's above the law*, not even me. So I says to that man, I says, 'I'll have you know I'm Mrs O'Demus, and my husband, Nic O'Demus, is on the leading council, so you'll watch what you say, thank you very much.'

I'm petrified, Mammy, what'll they do to him? They're not opposed to using the Romans to bump people off, that's no great secret. Nic believes this Jesus, I can tell. He told me he thinks he's been sent from God, and that he could be the Messiah. Which is a pretty big deal, isn't it?

Maybe you're right. Maybe he isn't brave enough to kick up a rumpus.

I don't know what I want him to do. Part of me wants him to follow his heart and make a stand. The rest of me wants to make sure nothing awful happens. We've got a family to think about. Oh, Mammy, I clean forgot to tell you in all the drama, that's why I rang. I'm expecting another.

I know, already! Eight weeks or so, I reckon.

Yeah, we're delighted. Looking forward to the miracle of another new life – there's nothing beats it, is there? Mind

you, now Nic'll be wanting it to live for ever!
So long as he doesn't make me deliver it twice!

Thanks, Ma, I will. Love you. Bye now.

(She addresses her tummy).

All right, baby, let's hope by the time you're born that
your daddy's made his mind up. Is he taking a risk and
throwing his lot in with this philosopher who could be
the Messiah? Or is he keeping his job and keeping
quiet? We'll see, won't we, eh?

Ach, life's a miracle, and I want you to get the most out
of it, wee thing. Maybe I should be deciding what I think
about the afterlife, for your sake. A life insurance policy
if nothing else. We might need it if Daddy carries this on.
(Sigh). We might need it.

Mrs Pilate

Pontius Pilate's wife is believed to have been called Claudia Procula, though much of her history is sketchy. In the Bible she is only mentioned once, in Matthew 27:19. She doesn't make a personal appearance, but a message she sends is relayed to her husband whilst he is conducting the trial of Jesus in his role as Roman Governor of the province. She asks Pilate to have nothing to do with Jesus, believing him innocent, and claims she's had a dream about him that has made her suffer greatly. There is a slightly longer account of the incident in The Acts of Pilate 2:1, in the New Testament Apocrypha. Here, Pilate relays her message to the Jewish leaders, who claim that they are aware of the fact that his wife 'Feareth God and favoureth rather the customs of the Jews.'

Many believe she was a follower of Jesus, and in fact she is canonized as a saint in the Greek Orthodox Church. More recently, she has also earned a special place in Roman Catholicism. A Latin letter believed to have been written by her was discovered in a monastery in Bruges, and is now referenced in the Vatican Archives. It was first translated into English and published in 1929. Although its authenticity is far from proven, it makes an interesting read. It claims she regretted Pilate's hand in the execution of Jesus, beginning with 'I am the wife of the man who condemned Jesus Christ to death' and ending her letter 'Ye who pray, pray now for Pontius.'[1] She refers to events recorded in the gospels, adding her own detail, even her own witnessing of Jesus' punishment. But she appears unaware of the resurrection, which means her horror at the death of Jesus is unmitigated and has none of the hope that inspires the New Testament account.

With limited information, I have embellished the details of her story. Although Mrs Pilate makes her star turn in Matthew, the springboard for this piece appears in the Gospel of John. In that account, Pilate concludes the trial with the question, 'What is truth?'[2] John seems to want us to notice that Pilate and Jesus shared a passion for that question. On the night before the crucifixion, he records Jesus declaring, 'I am the way, and the truth, and the life'[3] and earlier, 'If you hold to my teaching, you are really my disciples. Then you will know the truth, and the truth will set you free.'[4] How fascinating that Pilate has come face to face with a man claiming to be the answer to what he's searching for. How frustrating for his wife if she, seeing the connection, believes it is not given due attention.

It's likely she married around the age of fifteen, and I have imagined her remaining young and girlish in the absence of a need to mature until now. This is the moment she realizes she is an independent person with opinions of her own. She has experienced a lot today and is upset and unsettled by the dream she has had, unable to get it out of her mind. She is disturbed by the effect of events on her husband, and the possibility of their wider significance.

She loves her husband and has always relied on him. How will she feel about him now?

NOTES

[1]   At the time of writing, the full text of 'A Letter From Pontius Pilate's Wife' was available online:

http://www.archive.org/stream/letterfrompontiu
011959mbp/letterfrompontiu011959mbp_djvu.txt

[2] John 18:38.

[3] John 14:6.

[4] John 8:31,32.

No one takes kindly to a wailing wife in her nightwear storming the Governor's sitting. I might be passionate and emotional, but I'm not stupid. So I sent a messenger and gave him the exact words to say: 'Have nothing to do with that innocent man . . . I have suffered a great deal because of a dream about him.' I hoped it sounded striking enough, but not overdramatic. It was the truth. I knew he was innocent.

This morning was one of the mornings Pilate was gone when I woke, and I needed him. I was in a cold sweat and shaking. The pillow was so damp I think I'd been crying. It was a dream I'd never had before and hope I'll never have again.

I saw a man. A simple sort of man, but somehow perfect. Not like Pilate, not my sort of perfect, I mean he was . . . complete. He *did* what he said and he was what he said, and he was saying, 'I am the way, the truth and the life.' And I knew he was truth. But I couldn't see how he could be life because there was blood pouring out of him, out of his head, his back, his hands, his feet and his side, and how could all that blood be life? And the blood was pouring and pouring and covering everything and it was all over me and I forced myself to surface, to come round, and tried to think straight about what I'd seen.

Then I knew it was actually happening. That the man I'd seen was Jesus of Nazareth. And he was with Pilate right *now*. And he was innocent. And I had to do something to stop the blood because the thought of it staining Pilate was too much to bear.

I never interfere with his work. I watch sometimes or hide and listen, but I wouldn't pipe up. Who wants to hear a woman holding forth on something she's not required to comment on? But I've picked up a thing or two. I know I don't enjoy our stays in Jerusalem much. Especially when it's pilgrimage time and the city's crammed with everyone and his dog. The religious politics! Ugh. There's Herod and the High Priest and the chief priests and the Sanhedrin and the elders whipping up the crowd. Pilate referees – with Caesar to answer to. How on earth do you find the truth in that sort of soup?

And that's my Pilate's job; to know who to listen to, protect the empire and keep the peace. Hearing pleas, conducting trials, sitting on his judgement seat. My husband, the Prefect of Judea. I call him the Perfect of Judea; he frowns, but he secretly likes it. It's such a bore, hearing people go on about their other half, isn't it? As if they've no mind of their own. But I've never needed one. Pilate does the thinking for both of us.

He said the evidence wasn't just paper-thin, it was non-existent, but the defendant wasn't helping himself by speaking in riddles. 'Everyone who belongs to the truth listens to my voice.' I can just imagine Pilate's green eyes widening at that word that means so much to him. 'What is truth?' he'd asked. Not knowing he was looking at it.

I can't bear it. They'd brought Jesus in because they wanted him dead and, evidence or not, they were using my man to get what they wanted. The crowds were waiting and a riot was threatening, and a riot in Jerusalem is not good on the CV. So . . . he washed his hands. Told them he could find no case, but played the people-pleaser and allowed the execution. Is that something you can wash off your hands? The hands that will reach out to touch me tonight . . .

The *one* time I spoke out, the *one* time I told him what I thought about anything of any importance. The one time I cared about his work for any reason other than what it means to him. And all he did was wash his hands. God have mercy on him.

(A new thought). Why does it matter? Why do I care, when it's never bothered me before to be anything other than someone's lover? The lover of a man who's looking for the truth.

(A decision). Because I am not just his wife. My freedom will be to tell the truth and the truth will be my freedom. Even if Pilate banishes me from his side, which would be like losing half of myself, I will speak out.

Pilate just gave permission for the body to be taken down. He seemed surprised the request came so soon. The one who speaks truth is in his grave. Truth in a tomb. So what now?

Ms X

The criminals put to death on either side of Jesus are mentioned in Luke's account of the crucifixion. We know nothing about them except for the conversation they held with Jesus in their dying moments. The words of one, 'Jesus, remember me when you come into your kingdom',[1] are intriguing, particularly for an actor who must decide what drives a character to speak as they do. Jesus' reply is equally surprising: 'I tell you the truth, today you will be with me in paradise.'[2]

The word 'paradise' only appears in the Scriptures on two other occasions: it's mentioned by Paul in a claim that he was 'caught up' to paradise in a vision,[3] and in Revelation where it's described as the home of the tree of life.[4] This is the best type of life – eternal life. In other words, this is heaven.

It seems that, in the moments before he dies, the thief's acceptance of his own guilt and his trust in Jesus as the ruler of an eternal kingdom, have secured his place in it. The very idea would have outraged the religious Jews, who believed that salvation came through the very law this man had clearly neglected and abused throughout his life. (Not to mention the fact that Jesus, also condemned, felt able to promise admission to such a kingdom and referred to it as 'his'.)

The question of deathbed conversions bothers people to this day. Are they real? Are they fair? Is it just an insurance policy? There's a beautiful simplicity in the request of the thief to be remembered; to know, as his earthly life ends, that his existence is not entirely erased and meaningless. It reflects the paradox Jesus described of losing your life to keep it: '. . . the man who hates his life in this world will keep it for eternal life.'[5]

The girlfriend (or partner) of this criminal is entirely fictional, but there must have been many young men and women like her at the time, and still are today – guilty of breaking the law because they have no other means of survival.

I imagine this scene somewhere in East London. She is a hardened young girl with no options or opportunities, who finds herself in the first-century equivalent of a police cell. Ms X is her name because she is likely to be illiterate and, in running from the law, has reasons to be cagey about her identity. Although what she has witnessed today might just begin to affect that urge and need to run . . .

It hasn't been a good day. She saw her boyfriend executed, and was then arrested. She's tired of running. However, the conversation her boyfriend had with Jesus before his death has affected her, perhaps given her a glimmer of hope that being caught is not the end of the story.

NOTES

[1] Luke 23:42.
[2] Luke 23:43.
[3] 2 Corinthians 12:1–4.
[4] Revelation 2:7.
[5] John 12:25.

Criminal? Is that what you've got written at the top of that page? Well, that's not my name. I'll mark my X at the bottom of the page if you get the facts straight. I'm just a girl who gets hungry. I'm just a girl who lives with a guy who gets even more hungry than me. When his stomach is empty, his fists start flying. When mine is empty, I don't dodge as fast. When there's not enough to eat in our house, I get so clumsy my bruises seem to breed. So I make sure there's enough, however I can, to cut down my little accidents. But accidents happen.

Look, it's my life! What's it to you? We've been together for ages. We go together, no other option. I'm with him. He's with me. That's how it is.

Yeah, all right, *was*, how it *was*. Give me a break, it was only today.

I went because I wanted to see him – what do you think? I knew you'd be looking for me, but I couldn't leave him up there alone at the end, could I? What sort of person do you take me for? Don't answer that. I'm not ashamed. He was guilty, and he knew it.

I'd be more ashamed if I was shacked up with one of the Roman lackeys that killed him. They murder people day in, day out. Go and arrest *them*. Get this on the tape: Witness Statement. I saw a man hammering nails through the flesh of three men. I saw him watch and laugh as they gasped for air. I saw him stick a spear through the middle of one. Are you writing this down? I heard him say, 'Surely this man was the son of God,' and I thought, well you better keep your head down, mate, because you just killed him. I saw it, I saw it all, and you're bothering yourselves with the likes of me! Banged up for borrowing a few bits of bread, and loving some waster. A waster who's gone and got himself executed, got me caught into the bargain, and left me on my own to fight off the stinking pigs . . .

(There's a struggle).

No, wait, I'll calm down – not the restraints, please! I'll be good, I'm all right. What do you want me to say?

A confession? So you can get rid of me with a clear conscience?

Did you see what happened out there, before they were all dead and you grabbed me? They were shouting at the one in the middle, the one who had 'King of the Jews' on a sign above his head. The other guy, nasty piece of work – I think Jez knew him – was mocking him, saying a saviour should be able to save himself and the rest of them while he was at it. And Jez gets involved. Typical. Can't keep out of a fight. He shouts across, 'Even now, haven't you got the fear of God in you? We're getting what we've earned, but this guy's never done anything to deserve this.'

The justice system . . . Trial and retribution, isn't that what they call it? The guilty get their just deserts, and an innocent man gets put to death. So Jez looks over, and I don't know what made him say this, but it felt like the first honest thing he'd ever said, 'Jesus, remember me when you're ruling your kingdom!' I'm expecting a, 'Not on your life, mate!' but he manages a smile and says, 'I'm telling you, today you'll be with me in paradise.'

I'd like that.

He gets to go to paradise, today. I don't know what it looks like but it sounds like heaven, and I'm stuck in this hellhole with you.

(The insult riles her accusers).

Go on, hit me. I won't defend myself. Seems to me that life is one long effort to cheat death, and I'm too tired to try any more. Jez found his life just when he thought he'd lost it.

I have nothing to lose. Send me to trial. Let someone else choose what I deserve.

Are we done here?

Mrs Caiaphas

In the middle of Jerusalem stands the House of the Sadducees. It's now a museum displaying centuries-old artifacts, many from the time of Jesus. Behind one glass cabinet, along with her combs and bangles, is the make-up of the High Priest's wife – a lipstick and kohl pencil. That was the initial inspiration behind this piece.

The Jewish High Priest was chairman of the high court, with a duty to administer justice among his own people. (Religion and politics were one entity within the Jewish system. The leadership of the people consisted of the chief priests and the elders and the teachers of the law.) Caiaphas served as the Jewish High Priest for almost twenty years, following his father-in-law, Annas, who held the post for ten years. Several of Annas's sons were also high priests.[1] It was unusual for one family to dominate politics in this way. It seems Annas managed to ensure, by whatever means, that he was hugely influential through his family even after he was deposed.

It's surprising to note that it is Annas who questions Jesus after the arrest, before sending him to Caiaphas, who sends him to Pilate.[2] Caiaphas is also credited with instigating the plot to have Jesus killed.[3] Since they were unable to impose the death penalty, the Assembly of Judges handed over anyone thought deserving of capital punishment to the Roman authorities, claiming that they were a threat to Roman rule and empire. (Annas was later assassinated for advocating peace with Rome).

The High Priest lived in a palace with a courtyard (where Peter waits during the trial).[4] Despite the fact that her home was also the location of her husband's work, Mrs Caiaphas no doubt enjoyed the status and kudos of her position in society and the lifestyle that came with it, particularly as she had grown up with her father and brothers in the role. She is a fully qualified and long-standing WAG.

What people think of her (and of those she is with) is more important than anything else in her mind. She will paper over the cracks and keep smiling in public to make sure she always looks good. She organizes life to make sure nothing threatens her perfect reputation. Behind the scenes she will manipulate, fight, and do whatever she must, going to extreme lengths to protect her image. In this monologue, she is confiding a little more than she usually would. The pressure has loosened her tongue.

NOTES

[1]   Their terms of office were recorded by first-century historian, Josephus.
[2]   John 18:12–14,19–24.
[3]   John 11:47–53.
[4]   Matthew 26:3,57,58,69.

Isn't it funny how fast things can change? Yesterday was a good day, a great day. The first Sabbath of the Passover. I had a new outfit to show off – very chic; the High Priest's wife has to set certain standards. It's one of the *expectations*.

And you know how much work Passover is. Especially for the High Priest. And for the High Priest's wife. All that spring cleaning to remove every scrap of bread from the house. I'm exhausted. I paid my cleaner overtime. But we have to set an example. It isn't easy being married to the High Priest. Although I like the name . . . High Priest; sounds . . . important. But he works weekends, we live on the job, there's no escape and there are *expectations* – people think you're holy just because you live with him.

Anyway, yesterday went well; a good turn-out at the temple, takings up, spring on the way . . . and we had got rid of our chief troublemaker, that Nazarene, Jesus. Caiaphas and I began to pack for our holiday. Life was going my way. Yesterday.

Today, Caiaphas wasn't on duty. He'd fixed the rotas. Why have a dog and bark yourself? We went in late. To tell you the truth, we'd overdone the Passover spirit a bit, and were glad of a lie-in.

So there we were, strolling through the temple courts spreading goodwill, when my father appeared looking half-demented. I didn't think anything of it at first. After all, he's been married to my mother a very long time.

But then he yelped, 'What have you two got to look so happy about?' 'What isn't there to be happy about, Annas?' Caiphy asked him. 'Temple takings up, holiday starts tomorrow (a break away for two at the Waldorf on the beach at Caesarea) and, because it was Passover, we managed to bury the bad news and get rid of that pain in the proverbial, Jesus the Nazarene.'

'But that's just it, we haven't got rid of him,' Daddy said. Now I was really worried. 'It's all right, Daddy. We'll get you the best geriatrician in Jerusalem. That's why we've been paying into JUPA.'

'Annas,' said my long-suffering husband, 'we got him crucified. It usually does the trick. Then he was put in a tomb with a boulder in front. We checked, remember? And we posted guards, Romans from Pilate's garrison, to make sure there was no funny business.'

'But that's just it,' my father wailed. 'The guards were as much use as a pig at the Passover. The tomb's open and the body's gone, oy veh!' He was kicking up such a rumpus, he could be heard all the way across Jerusalem! What an embarrassment . . . Yelling and pulling at my dress. I wish I'd worn my French Connection and kept the Versace for Pentecost.

I took him home. Keeping the peace is one of the *expectations*. Meanwhile, Caiphy saw the guards. Apparently they babbled about earthquakes and angels and that Jesus had risen from the dead and there were plenty who'd testify. What is happening to the forces, I ask you?

Caiphy told them that if the Governor got word they'd had a little snooze on the job and the disciples had stolen the body, then we'd cover for them. They understood him when his wallet came out. That's more like it.

But it's not over yet: Tertius, the centurion, the one Caiphy posted at the cross (built like an Adonis, normally very dependable, very willing and very discreet), has taken leave of his senses. Believes this ridiculous resurrection story and is telling the entire world. He won't be bribed. He's going the right way to get himself sacked, if not martyred. Just give us long enough to think up the charges . . . Problem is, we'll need charges for every one of these witnesses crawling out of the woodwork claiming they've seen the infidel alive. It's all part of maintaining law and order. It's one of the *expectations*.

I could do without all this stress when I'm so busy. I'm having a pedicure at three, my hair done at four, nails at five, and I've booked an hour on the sunbed at six. Now I'll have to see my therapist as well. Honestly! I'm really going to need that holiday by the time Caiphy has sorted this little lot. I did not sign up for this. There are limits. Dealing with dead men disappearing is not one of the *expectations*.

Mrs Zebedee

James and John are the sons of Zebedee: they are brothers from Galilee, called to follow Jesus while fishing, and they end up as two of the inner three in his band of disciples. In Matthew 20:20–28, their mother turns up to ask Jesus a favour – the story recounted here.

In their accounts of the crucifixion and resurrection, the four gospels differ in their records of who was where at what point, and confuse us with those who share names. To create Mrs Zebedee, aspects of the four gospel accounts are combined, particularly noting that there were women who toured with the disciples and provided for them financially;[1] that 'the mother of the sons of Zebedee' was present at the crucifixion;[2] and that a woman called Salome, also present at the crucifixion, accompanied Mary Magdalene to the tomb.[3] So we have made Salome and Mrs Zebedee the same person, as some scholars have suggested may be the case.

Mrs Zebedee takes life as it comes, and throws herself into it. She is matronly, a good Jewish mama with a matter-of-fact sense of humour, who wants only the best for her children. She's certainly not stupid and doesn't suffer fools gladly. She may well be baking or knitting. She's just got back to Galilee from the Passover pilgrimage to Jerusalem. She's talking to her friend Sadie, who missed out on the trip and the events of the first

Easter. It works well with a Yiddish twang if you can manage one!

She is reliving the things she recounts as she speaks, visualizing each moment. But there is a light touch to the sad moments because she already knows the resurrection has happened.

NOTES

1   Mark 15:41.
2   Matthew 27:56.
3   Mark 15:40; Mark 16:1.

Oy, has it been a week. The pain in my feet, I can't tell you.

Where to begin, Sadie, I just don't know. It's been so long since I've seen you properly. Three years, is it? I hear it was your shift at home this year.

Yes, we're all back from Jerusalem now. Passover's done and am I glad to see Galilee again! For one thing, I'm sick of the Romans calling me Salami. I said, 'It's Salome, not Salami, you sausage. What Jew would be called Salami? Get the name right – *Salome*, it means "peace".'

Not that I've had much! I always thought I'd have more once the boys were grown. James and John were such a handful, a couple of tearaways, always in trouble. Their father and I wondered if they'd ever amount to much.

Till the day they were all out fishing together, and Zeb comes home alone and says the two of them were hand-picked by a rabbi to be his disciples. I laughed in his face. My boys don't have the education to train with a rabbi. 'Jesus told them they'll be fishing for people,' Zeb said. Whatever that means, I thought.

'Sons of Thunder', Jesus calls them. He likes to tease. And he's channelled all that thunder into pure sunshine. Am I proud, Sadie? Beaming!

Well, you know that after Zeb passed on, the business saw me well provided for, thank you very much, so I decided to go with them; follow the troupe around and keep an eye on my boys. Funny thing, though, in the end it was Jesus I kept my eye on. Couldn't keep my eyes off him. That man can turn you inside out with a look. A look that makes you feel pure – like one hundred per cent wool. It was a joy to feed him. 'Salome,' he used to say, 'there's no one makes chicken soup like you. But don't tell my mother I said so.' Mary. Such a blessing to have a son like that.

He and I had a bit of banter; I felt we were close. So, one day I asked him a favour. By that time I was pretty sure he was going places, you know, Messiah-style. So I asked if James and John could sit either side of him when he was king in his glorious kingdom. He nearly died laughing. I wasn't smiling. 'Ever the Jewish mama, Salome,' he said. And what else would a Jewish mama want for her boys but the best? A straight yes or no would've done. 'You don't get it,' he said. 'Whoever wants to be great has to be a servant, just as yours truly came to serve, and give his life as a ransom for many.' No, I didn't get it. Not all that 'giving up your life' business. Depressing talk for such a lovely boy.

I nagged him: 'Why don't you rest?' At the beck and call of whoever needed him, welcoming the crowds, mixing with the riff-raff, healing people, preaching as if his heart would burst. 'You'll work yourself into an early grave,' I said. Why did I waste my breath? We all tried to persuade him not to go to Jerusalem for the Passover.

Oh, that terrible moment when I stood at the cross with Mary. Watching the awful death of the most beautiful man who ever lived. When he turned to my John and asked him to adopt Mary as a second mother, I thought my heart would break. Always thinking of everyone but himself.

This was only last week, Sadie! Feels like a lifetime.

He was buried just before Sabbath came in.

Sunday morning, two days on, Mary Magdalene wants to anoint his body with spices, but says she's spooked, will I go and hold her hand? I ask you, the woman who once incapacitated half the Roman army! She says live men she can handle, dead ones – she's not so keen. I said, 'Joseph of Arimathea larded him with preservatives already. You can't do any more for him, love.' But she was off.

We're halfway there when she says, 'What about the stone?' 'What stone?' says I. 'The one-ton lump of concrete at the entrance.' I snorted: 'You could have thought of that before, I'd have brought my Black and Decker.'

Otherwise, it was an uneventful journey – oh, except for an earthquake. Dodging the flying rubble, I said, 'Mary, for an outing, this was a wonderful day.' 'Don't be a crazy old woman,' she says, so I shot back, 'My body may be in ruins, young lady, but there's nothing wrong with my mind.'

So what do we find when we get there? That we needn't have worried. The earthquake's dislodged the stone, and there's just a gaping hole where it had been. It's a tomb with a view.

There's a boy inside, dressed from head to toe in white. I said, 'I bet your mother doesn't like you wearing that, the washing must be endless. Is she some sort of saint?' He says, 'I'm an angel.' I said, 'Don't flatter yourself – she may think you are, but I'm not taken in.'

'Her body may be in ruins, but there's nothing wrong with her mind,' says Mary Mags, and I nod for empha-sis. And he snaps back, 'Then why are you looking in a grave for someone who's alive? He's not here, he's risen like he said he would. Go and tell the boys, and send them back to Galilee, where they'll see him.'

I double-checked inside the tomb. I wasn't born yesterday . . . as Zeb always used to remind me. Jesus wasn't there all right, just the marks where he'd been – and a neatly folded shroud. Always a tidy man, I'll say that for him.

Mary was wailing and I could feel a migraine coming on – so we made to head for home. I wanted to tell the boys quick smart. But we stopped when we heard a voice behind us. 'Psst, Mary!' It's only him, isn't it? 'Jesus!' I said. 'I wish you wouldn't do that kind of thing. I nearly jumped out of my *kishkes*.' I couldn't scold him. I couldn't stop laughing – for the joy of seeing him standing there. Meanwhile, Mary's thrown herself on his feet, weeping – she's the emotional type.

He sent us off to tell the lads. She had me as close to running as I've been in years. Nearly killed me – but was it worth it? Oy! Bless them.

What my Sons of Thunder might get up to with a risen and back-from-the-dead-type Messiah as a best friend, I can only imagine. Watch this space, I tell you. My James and John will be on his right and left, sitting or standing, or flat on their faces.

Because if he's the Messiah, and I tell you, Sadie, we've pretty good reason to suspect he is, then we'll all be with him in glory, won't we? So, I wasn't that far out after all. I've said it before and I'll say it again, my body may be in ruins, but there's nothing wrong with my mind!

Mrs Didymus

Thomas Didymus is better known as 'Doubting Thomas'. It seems a bit unfair that this apostle is remembered for his one moment of disbelief, rather than for all the other adventures of faith he pursued headfirst.

Most people can relate to his thirst for tangible evidence of the resurrection. No one is keen to be seen as gullible, or wants to be taken for a ride. The laws of nature are not usually overturned, and it's not easy when the spiritual realm challenges what we instinctively know and believe. Perhaps that's why Thomas's honest moment of fame is so reassuring.

There are people who want hard facts; there are others who go on gut feelings. Most of us use some combination of the two, even if we lean more towards one than the other. In Hebrews, Paul writes that 'faith is being sure of what we hope for and certain of what we do not see.'[1] A bit of evidence does wonders for inspiring that faith, nonetheless. Thomas is given the verification he craves, and then Jesus tells him, 'blessed are those who have not seen and yet have believed.'[2]

Perhaps his wife came into that latter category. Maybe she was someone who was able to believe what was corroborated by witnesses, without needing first-hand evidence. It doesn't make her any less practical or grounded. She's a down-to-earth woman who knows her mind and is prepared to speak it. Being faith-filled makes her a little more gentle than she might otherwise be. There's warmth in her chiding.

Whilst having a quiet drink, she overhears an argument that she can't help butting into. The lesson she has learned in life, she wants to share.

NOTES

[1]   Hebrews 11:1.
[2]   John 20:29.

Excuse me, I can't help overhearing your 'conversation'. I wasn't eavesdropping, but you're talking quite loud and this is a small establishment. Maybe if I can help solve your problem, then we can all go back to a quiet drink.

I hear you insisting that the evidence doesn't add up. Well, I disagree. I see facts aplenty on this one. But more to the point, truth isn't made up of physical proofs alone. At some point you have to believe a witness statement. You can't be everywhere. I've tried being omnipresent, and I just end up all over the place. My husband is a man who likes to deal in hard facts, so I understand their worth, believe me. But I can tell you, I've learnt a thing or two about evidence.

Sorry, I should've introduced myself. I'm Mrs Didymus, but they call me Diddy for short. Diddy – for short! I've been that since I married Thomas. He's a big man, my Tom. Didymus means 'twin'. They're identical. Used to cause some confusion in the early days. I once kissed him passionately – in the marketplace – only to discover it was the wrong man. How embarrassing is that? He told me to deal in hard facts: he has a birthmark on his neck that his brother doesn't. 'Indisputable evidence,' he'd say.

I prefer to go with my instincts, and I was usually right . . . Anyway, the problem was solved when they parted ways, which was when Tom went on tour. For three years he went all around the Galilee, to Jerusalem and back, up mountains, down valleys, over the hills and far away, wherever Jesus went. 'Doesn't surround himself with yes men, this Jesus,' I said to him, 'if he'll have you as one of his disciples.'

My Tom says it how it is. Never been backward at coming forward. And he was completely taken with this rabbi, vowed to follow him for the rest of his life. In fact, it got to the point where he vowed to follow him until death did them part. I told him, 'Oi! That's my prerogative!' Apparently it's different. You make exceptions for someone who has given that amount of evidence that he's the Messiah.

I remember the day Jesus told them he was heading back to Judea to heal Lazarus. We all tried to dissuade him. He would be too late anyway, and the authorities were out to get him. It was madness to put himself at risk, and we told him so. Except Tom, who pipes up, 'Let's all go and we can die with him!' Awkward silence. Jesus smiled and squeezed his shoulder. But I pulled him aside and said, 'Thanks a lot, Tom! What about me and the kids? What'll we do if you get yourself killed?' 'Oh,' he said, and his big face fell. 'Oh, I never thought. It's just . . . I think I'd rather die with him than live without him.' I held my tongue and put my arms around him instead. I don't think there'd be many wives that understanding.

It took every ounce of understanding I had to see him through his grief amidst my own, when they took the

Messiah and crucified him, the idiots! Tom's whole world fell apart. He was broken-hearted. I couldn't reach him. No one could comfort him. He didn't even want to be with the rest of the lads. He just wanted to be left alone.

So when they turned up a couple of days later saying they'd seen Jesus, that he was risen from the dead, Tom drove them out of the house, shouting: 'You're being deceived, wishful thinking, hallucinating! Unless I see him with my own eyes and touch him with my own hands, I'll never believe it. I want hard evidence of the wounds I saw inflicted. I need substantiation!' Big word for Thomas, that.

He went on for eight days. Eight days, ranting and raving about dealing in hard facts. Eventually I couldn't stand it any longer. You know what men are like. I had a bear with a sore head under my feet all day. I couldn't get anything done. So I persuaded him to go and touch base with the others, fight it out if nothing else. See if they could pray.

Jesus just appeared in the room. Locked doors no object. He went straight to my man and said, 'Hey, Tom, want to touch the nail marks in my hands and feel the spear scar in my side? Go on, you know you do – you keep telling the world you do! Give me your hand, feel here . . . now, what do you reckon?'

Thomas fell to his knees and tried to speak. All he could say was, 'My Lord and my God!' It was a moment to behold. Apparently. The others were laughing fit to burst.

It's typical of me to miss the crucial moment. I'm miffed I didn't see Jesus for myself. But not because I feel a desperate need for hard facts and evidence.

You know, I can tell my Tom from his brother now with my eyes closed or open, birthmark or not. I know him so well that my instincts serve me. And this Jesus thing is like that. I didn't need to see him to know he'd risen. But I wanted to because I'd love to see him in the flesh just one more time. Apparently, Jesus said to Tom, 'You believe because you've seen me. But let me tell you how blessed are those who haven't seen me in the flesh, but believe anyway.'

So, what does that make me? A very blessed woman, that's what. Blessed.

And I'll be even more blessed if you two can pipe down and let me finish my pint in peace. All right?

Mrs Peter

Peter is something of a Christian giant, one of Jesus' closest friends and often described as the father of the church. He appears throughout the gospels and the Acts of the apostles, in Paul's letters, and in two of his own.

There are so many ways of approaching Peter's story. This piece covers some of the richest moments, mostly from later in the story. It could be edited into shorter episodes to highlight a particular incident.

It is Peter's reputation as the founder of the church that is the focus, centred around the moment he becomes a preacher at Pentecost.[1] It's a fearless, faultless sermon and a startling revelation for a man who so far has been known as much for his blundering as for his moments of brilliance.

Paul writes, 'Don't we have the right to take a believing wife along with us, as do the other apostles . . . and Cephas?'[2] Cephas is translated 'Peter' and, from other references,[3] this would appear to be the same person. From this we've accepted his wife travelled with him. It was already clear that he was married because Jesus had healed his mother-in-law.[4]

Here, Peter's wife is a lovable, talkative, larger than life northern lass with a great story to tell, and tell it she will. Listener or no, Mrs Peter will speak out, as much to process events for herself as to pass the time of day. She understands

Peter's commission completely, and is excited to be with him. She is honest, open and entertaining. Given the chance, she would probably make a good preacher herself.

At this moment her husband is preaching, and she has found a place in the shade to wait, probably by a well where she can drink and will have a ready audience of passers-by.

NOTES

1   Acts 2:1–42.
2   1 Corinthians 9:5.
3   John 1:42.
4   Matthew 8:14,15.

It's a bit sweaty in Antioch, isn't it? Tropical! I didn't know I would miss Jerusalem so much. Not that I'm complaining; I'm glad to be here. Can't quite believe it; me, a world traveller! Me mum would laugh.

Sorry?

Oh, no, that's OK, don't worry yourself, my Turkish is rubbish.

I've come here with him. That one up there doing all the talking.

Oh, don't you be deceived by that stocky build. He's not a brave man – my Peter. Might like to think he is, but he'd never done owt brave till he stepped out onto the water. But then, Jesus were holding his hand, so I don't think that counts. The night he kept telling that barmaid he'd never even known Jesus reminded him of his mettle. Lack of. And she were only a slip of a thing, sniggering behind her hand.

He were gutted. Well, you would be, wouldn't you? When you know the Messiah and you blank him when he needs you most. I poked fun at him later, God forgive me. 'You remember Jesus – the man who healed your manic mother-in-law, got the woman up off her sickbed to cook him his tea?' I mean, you don't forget a man like that, do you? Nor did *she*.

When I used to tell her that Peter were practically living with Jesus, that he preferred him to me, she'd say, 'Shut up whingeing, will you. It's given him summat to live for. It'll make a man of him.' Well, just look at him now. He's a man all right, and a good 'un. Looked to me like he turned into a man that day he held forth for the first time. It wasn't long after they all had breakfast on the beach with Jesus when he were back from the dead.

Jesus had gone past the denial debacle, made a fresh start, and given Pete a mission. A mission and a half. Pete vowed he'd make it up to him, and by 'eck, is he ever. He's ready to prove himself a worthy foundation for the Jesus movement. (When Jesus called him a solid rock I told him, 'Well, I've always said you're a great lump. It's nice to have it confirmed.')

Anyway, here's you gasping for the details. Let me get to the good bit. Right, so, temple courts were packed out for the spring festival. Thousands there from all over the shop, eating, drinking and having a right knees-up, like you do at Pentecost. Out of nowhere there were this almighty roar – a force ten gale, no word of a lie. Knocked some of us clean off our feet onto the floor. I felt as if I were on fire. I thought I were having an early menopause – until I saw that all of us Jesus followers were in the same state – visibly burning, a lick of flame on our heads, and gabbling in languages we'd never learnt. There were plenty visitors who understood, though – we were singing psalms to God in their languages, apparently. It sounded beautiful but it were a bit of a shocker. Some of the locals – the posher lot, who've been to school and like everything controlled and dignified, said it were the new wine had made us legless, and what could you expect from a bunch of northern wasters.

Well, that did it. He leapt to his feet. My Peter! The one who makes *me* get rid of the spiders. And he told them in no uncertain terms we were not 'inebriated' – it were far too early in the morning for that. And then he kept speaking.

Honest to God, I don't know where the words came from, but he preached a blinder. He told 'em straight – that this was all forecast in the prophets, in Joel and in David. That Jesus is the long-promised Messiah, and it were time to turn around and believe in him so they could receive this Holy Spirit they were seeing in action. And then get world-changing for generations to come. Before he'd even got to the end, there were three thousand queuing for baptism. You've never seen owt like it for an altar call. If I'd have sold tickets, I'd have made a fortune.

I were as proud as punch and beaming. He were so bold, so clear – so charismatic. This was the same impetuous, headstrong – and let's be honest, mildly idiotic – lad I married, who vowed he'd change the world one day. And now he has.

He's preaching everywhere, as you see. And healing folk all over the place. Doing all the miracles he saw

Jesus do, and more. He can't stop. Even though the authorities hate it and it's getting him into trouble. Scares me.

They've thrown him in prison already. A bunch of us met to pray for him to be let out. We were intercessing fit to burst. There were a knock on the door and Rhoda goes and opens it, sees it's him and slams it in his face. Well, you don't expect your prayers answered that quick, do you? After buzzing and praising God we got round to letting him in. 'Bloomin' 'eck,' he says. 'It's easier to get out of prison than into one of your prayer meetings.' He were grinning though, said it were an angel let him out. *(She makes a face)*.

The old Peter was safer. Duller maybe.

Sometimes I want those days back. There, I've said it.

Trusting God is easier said than done when you're watching your hubby striding to an early grave. He holds my face and says, 'Sweetheart, didn't I say I'd make it up to Jesus? This is what he told me I'd do – I'm feeding his sheep.' He were never into metaphors till he met Jesus. Feeding sheep. I suppose it's not a bad way to describe people. Mostly mucky, mooching about, and needing someone to follow.

He's done Samaria, Lydda, Joppa. I've packed his case plenty of times. This time it's further afield. More danger.

Places I haven't even dreamt of. He says, 'There's millions of 'em out there, if I could just lay me hands on them.'

I told him, you don't need to preach to me, I'm on the same page, so can I come with? Well, if you can't beat 'em . . .

I were nagging a bit before we set off. He said to me, 'You know when he put the wind up us at Pentecost? I reckon there's plenty more where that came from.'

So that's how I ended up here, in this Turkish bath. Well, not *in* the bath of course! Bit of a joke, you get me? (*She laughs at the joke*). On account of it being so hot? (*Her listener doesn't seem to get it, so she continues*).

First stop Antioch, next stop no idea. If I expect an adventure, I'll be ready. Bring it on, and God help us.

Goodness, the sun's going down and I'm still yakking on. You poor love, you must have places to be. Yes, off you go, don't let me keep you. Bye, love, take care.

Right, let me grab that husband of mine. Talking gives him such an appetite, and I'm famished.

Mrs John

Revelation is probably the most difficult book in the Bible for a contemporary audience to understand. It's worth noting that in its original form, the Bible was not expected to be studied alone. It would have been read aloud and discussed. Comprehension would have therefore been a great deal easier. It was also written within a cultural frame of reference and context that listeners would have understood.

Anyone reading Revelation benefits from background information on the literature and symbolism of the time. Armed with that knowledge, the metaphors become as accessible to the contemporary reader as they were to the original recipients of the letter. I'm grateful to the Revd Dr Ian Paul for his book, How to Read the Book of Revelation[1] *which proved inspirational on the many occasions when I couldn't grasp what the apostle John was trying to say.*

Many theologians agree that Revelation is not a futuristic vision of earth, but a description of the way the world currently is. The final chapters describe the way it will be one day, when it is redeemed. Interestingly, heaven is not a place to which believers will be removed, rather God comes to dwell on earth, restoring it to what it is meant to be.

The Bible has come full circle, and yet it has moved on. All God's promises from the beginning of time will be fulfilled. *The evil serpent, that brought such misery to Mrs Adam and her descendants, that wrought such havoc in the world, has been conquered once and for all by one of her offspring – a triumphant Christ, risen, ascended and reigning for ever over the people who have longed for his coming. Only now the garden, never static in its development, has become a city where there is only light, joy and celebration.*

Mrs John is a figment of my imagination. At this time the Roman Emperor Nero was persecuting and murdering the new believers, as other emperors went on to do. John is a prisoner for his faith, condemned to hard labour on the island of Patmos, a Roman penal colony. The enforced separation must have been hard to bear and she tears open his letter, expecting to hear about inadequate food and harsh conditions, not an extraordinary vision of hope and victory. The pictures aren't as obscure to her as they sometimes seem to us. She understands exactly what her husband is telling her. One day, oppressive empires will fall, and the persecution of the saints will be over for ever. There will be no more pain or suffering, sorrow or separation, injustice or death. Like the rest of the beleaguered and oppressed new church, or anyone persecuted for their beliefs, she must hold on in faith, and wait with patience for the fulfilment of the heavenly vision.

She has John's letter (the text of Revelation, with a cover note) in her hand. She may refer to it or read from it as she speaks. Although she is not a young woman, she is youthful in her worldview. Her vitality comes across well in a West Country accent.

It would be easy to make this piece sound sentimental and cheesy. Instead, she needs to remain matter-of-fact and earthy. There is a tension between being filled with hope by the vision, and living in a place where it is not yet a reality.

NOTE

1 Ian Paul, *How to Read the Book of Revelation* (Cambridge: Grove Books, 2005), www.grovebooks.co.uk.

(She has a large document in her hand).

The instant this arrived I came over all prickly, like I'd just jumped in a cold plunge. It was the sight of his familiar scrawl. The relief of knowing he's alive.

That man has brought me nothing but worry. Peter was crucified upside down. Then Paul was beheaded, leaving John top of the hit list. I begged him to hide. But you might as well try to hold back Niagara as stop John preaching. They took him – my sweet old John – across the sea to Patmos. A Greek island, you smile, what can be so bad? But Patmos isn't all Retsina and hummus. It's manacles that eat the flesh of your wrists and ankles.

Who would subject an old man in frail health to hard labour? But that's our Roman masters for you. They're pro-faith, pro-spirituality, pro-anything you want to believe in, so long as it's not Jesus. If that's who you follow, the emperor wants you torn apart for sport.

I haven't seen my John for years. I was beginning to panic that we've had no contact, but why did I fear? It seems he's been busy writing the longest letter known to man, or his wife.

He sounds surprisingly upbeat for a man in exile. 'The food could be better and the facilities aren't great, especially in such stinking hot weather. But on the plus side,

I've plenty of time for prayer.' That man could find the silver lining in the steaming dung of a sick goat.

The local believers creep around here every day for word of him. They're desperate for any advice he might send about how to share the good news with people who would rather torture you than hear what you have to say. Jesus did warn us this is how it would be. Not that that makes it any easier.

John asks would I mind having the enclosed letter copied seven times by someone trustworthy and sent on to the seven churches listed? The whole thing is a vision . . . I thought at first 'hallucination' was more like it. I wondered if the isolation was finally getting to him. Either that or he'd had too much Greek sun. All these fantastical creatures and dizzying storylines. Someone must've been reading him *Lord of the Rings*. But I can't write it off, it ties up all the threads too coherently. It's vintage John. He's always had a penchant for the poetic. There's his usual treasure hunt of numbers and riddles. He knows I've never been a whiz at cryptic crosswords and I'm a slowcoach at Sudoku, but this time I get his gist.

I know who 666 is without having to think: our great imperial oppressor. He doesn't come off all that well; the Almighty steals his glory and trumps his red-carpet worship. If he gets wind of this, he'll be baying for blood. I don't want to face that now, even if he is subject to eternal judgement afterwards.

Mind you, we already are facing it. Whores, drunkenness, beasts and fire pits, it sounds just like town on a Friday night.

Poverty, earthquakes and full-on war; all that we hear in the evening news. And it goes on to power lust, famine, death and financial crisis. We paint a sorry picture.

But, right in the midst of the mess, just when you think it can't get any worse, there's a revelation. Get this: Jesus is coming back! And he's dressed up for the occasion! He comes in blazing with a mighty soundtrack like an action hero, and corruption and death get trounced once and for all. *(She shouts)*. Freedom!

As soon as that's sorted, can you Adam and Eve it, God comes to live with us, here on earth! A brand-spanking-new world. Then we'll be able to forget how it is now, because it's going to be . . . *(Long exhale/whistle)*.

God? Living down here? With us? He's going to have to do a pretty big renovation job to want to move in. But he does. Listen, 'God himself will be with them . . . He will wipe every tear from their eyes, death will be no more, mourning and crying and pain will be no more.'

Which isn't a happy ending, is it? It's a new beginning. A repossession of the beautiful way things started out. And this place will shine like it was made to, and so will we.

I've read it right through ten times already since this morning. It's a page-turner. Bestseller, you watch. I just know everyone will read it and say, 'So that's what's going on. I totally get it now.'

(She puts the letter down and picks up a baby).

Yesterday I was about ready to give up and give in. I wasn't top of the faith-filled pile, dwelling on all this fear of death stuff, not knowing if John will ever get our news, that we have a grandchild.

But now I can hear his voice, 'We're united in patient endurance.' Slightly optimistic of him; I've never been that patient. I'm desperate to see him and hold him and know he's in one piece. And show him this little girl. One of a new generation who might take John's message a great deal further than Greece. So I won't lose hope – not now.

Hold on, John. If this vision's anything to go by, trial and perseverance will be worth it when we're reunited. In this Jerusalem, or in the one to come.

Acknowledgements

We would like to thank all the people who have inspired us, supported us, encouraged and helped us: in particular David and Wendy Lewis, J John at The Philo Trust, Steve Stickley at Footprints Theatre Trust, Elin Kelly at Lacey Theatre Company www.laceytheatrecompany.com and not least Peter, Joel and Sarah Guinness. We also appreciate all those who have ever offered us a stage and opened the doors for us to experiment.

In particular, we acknowledge the late Rob Lacey (author of *The Word on the Street*, formerly *The Street Bible*) without whom this book probably wouldn't exist. He is much loved and sorely missed.

About the Authors

Abby Guinness was caught, aged three, speaking into a mirror and replying in a host of character accents. She has ever since been acting up, highlighted by a short stint as Anne in *The Diary of Anne Frank* at The Grand Theatre in Lancaster. She trained in English Literature and Drama at Sheffield University and The Royal Welsh College of Music and Drama and has worked as an actress in a wide variety of roles. She was in Riding Lights Theatre Company and was later a founding member of Lacey Theatre Company, where, under the guidance of Rob Lacey, she began to write more. In addition to performing, she now writes, directs, teaches and facilitates. You can find out more at www.livingandactive.co.uk. As well as her work in theatre, Abby appears at a range of events and conferences. She spent over two years on the staff of Holy Trinity Brompton as Arts Director, and is now Head of Creative Arts for Spring Harvest.

Michele Guinness studied French and Drama at Manchester University. She is a prolific author and has worked as a presenter, researcher and writer for national TV and radio. She speaks at events all over the country including Spring Harvest, New Wine, Detling and Words

by the Water, Keswick. Her recent books include, *Chosen,
The Heavenly Party* and *Autumn Leave.*